QUEERING
CONSTELLATIONS

MAPPING THIS JOURNEY CALLED LIFE

RAJA GOPAL BHATTAR

Tehom Center Publishing is a 501(c)3 nonprofit publishing feminist and queer authors, with a commitment to elevate BIPOC writers. Its face and voice is Rev. Dr. Angela Yarber.

Paperback ISBN: 978-1-966655-03-9

Ebook ISBN: 978-1-966655-06-0

CONTENTS

*To all those making
constellations out of chaos
and finding peace against all odds.
You are manifesting the sacred pathways
to your own wonderful bliss.*

ACKNOWLEDGMENTS

Breathing in, I am in this present moment,
Breathing out, I am grateful for my beloved community.

Truly, the cultivation of this book has been a community effort. I am grateful for so many kind souls that have inspired and encouraged me over the years. I am thankful for my spiritual guides, ancestors and the Universal Shakti for ushering me towards fully living my own truth. This book would not be possible without my month-long retreat in a gorgeous cabin in the mountains of Big Bear thanks to the generosity of Mama Hooks and Karen Hooks. From virtual coworking dates with Dr. Chantal Weaver and Dr. Jinann Bitar to processing ideas with Dr. Lilith Mahmud, Dr. Joy and Dr. John Hoffman (and Jackson), my community has been gracious beyond my imagination. While these stories have been in my heart for decades, my editor, the Book Doula Rev. Dr. Angela Yarber, listened to my wild visions for this book and brought constant enthusiasm and support for this process. Throughout this journey, Allison McComb, Dr. Charity Bowles, Dr. Chantal Weaver, Calla Goldberg, Yetunde Janski-Ogunfidodo and others have read pieces or entire drafts and provided invaluable insights, and I'm so thankful for each of them! Thanks to D'Lo, Dr. Bobby Kunst-man, Dr. Sunny Lee, Dr. Al Day, Dr. Preeti Sharma, Justin Gerboc, and so many others for providing constant encouragement throughout this process. Finally, I am deeply grateful for Chandra (the Moon), Surya (the Sun) and the celestial Nakshatras (stars) for reminding me that we shine, not in spite of the pain but because of the healing fire we carry within us.

QUEERING CONSTELLATIONS MAP

INTRODUCTION

My dear friend -

I'm grateful this book has landed exactly where it was meant to be... with you.

By just opening this book, we are in community together.

Our stories intertwined, our paths crossing.

Thank you for being part of my story and for making me part of yours. I cannot wait to witness your truth in these pages. I have come to believe that there are no coincidences in life and that people and experiences come in or leave from our lives when we have a lesson to learn. Nothing in life is a mistake. Each event is a precise moment of learning and sometimes (often!) relearning until we understand the lesson.

This book is an offering. A prayer. A vision.

I've been wanting to write this book for years but as a young English Language Learner (ELL) who was made to repeat first grade as soon as I got to the United States because of my English skills, I have held onto some of that trauma to this day. I've always struggled with using my voice to tell my story. Is my English good enough? Does my story matter? Will it make sense to anyone else? I'm sure many of us have had these questions in life. I offer this memoir to each of you and to the Universe. May this story resonate with you, make you laugh at points and maybe even inspire teary-eyes. May this journey ultimately reconnect you with your own story.

Our stories are sacred, our journeys divine.

My story is no greater or lesser than yours. Our greatest resource is our story and our greatest barrier is our notion of what our story is supposed to be. Recognizing that time is both everlasting and yet limited can be our greatest liberation. Our recognition that we may not have forever, but we have today. We have this moment. I get to breathe right now. And I don't even have to think about it!

How will you read this book? What will you add from your story? How can we co-constellate a better reality for all of us?

I come from a long lineage of Indian storytellers, from my Thatha who told us mythologies of wars between gods and demons, my Amma telling me stories of growing up in a small town while having to walk three miles each day to school, or my sister recounting all the latest family drama over the phone. I remember as a young child, my Amma would sit all of my cousins and me in a circle late into the evening as she mixed Hulianna (Sambar rice) and distributed them to us in perfectly rounded scoops at a time. She would recount stories of the Hindu god Krishna's mischievous childhood pranks or the greatness of Vanake Obowa, a Kannada woman from the 1700s who single-handedly fought off an invading army with just a large pestle from her kitchen.

This and my earliest memories all take place at 200 Bhestara Bheedhi, our 200-year old, thick mud-walled, multi-generational home where every day was an adventure. In the center of the house was a large common room that served as a dining hall, gathering spot for celebrations, family meetings and story-filled meals. This is where people would come to visit my Thatha to ask for help with matching horoscopes, organize religious events, or inquire about some esoteric Sanskrit text that he could somehow always identify and contextualize among his many brown paper bound books lining the back of his room. Above the patchy pale blue chalk paint, I remember the pictures that hung on each side of the room, like a court jury overlooking all the happenings of the hall. At least thirty large gold frames hung close to the ceiling at an angle that it felt like they could fall down at any moment. Each was filled with black and white paintings, color photos or drawings of various gods, goddesses, ancestors, and recently dead relatives; all adorned with a mix of fresh jasmine strands and dusty plastic floral garlands. Walking in through the old wooden doors, heavy with at least a dozen coats of paint, felt like walking into a museum or judgment hall.

"That woman is your Thatha's great grandmother," says my sister, just two years older than me but she feels so much older to my four-year old self. "And those your great grand-parents and these two were the extended family that adopted Thatha since they had no children of their own and that is a picture of Krishna, our family god, and that a drawing of a temple where Thatha used to work, and that... " And on and on she went, identifying each frame with such confidence that it felt like I was on an official museum tour. That moment was my first introduction to my ancestral lineages and the importance of remembering these people who died long before my time, but are essential to me being alive. Since the age of four I've been fascinated with who my ancestors are and what it means that I will someday be an ancestor. What stories will be told, if any?

In my own education and coming out experience, my self-identity depended on learning about living and dead queer and transcestry: Audre Lorde, Gloria Anzaldúa, James Baldwin, Bayard Rustin, Alexander the Great, Laverne Cox, Ellen DeGeneres, Rock Hudson, Frida Kahlo, Leslie Feinberg, Matthew Shepard, and so many others. I would spend hours at the public library, perusing books and websites with lists of "Top 100 LGBTQ leaders' ' or "Historical Gay Figures", and so on. I never saw myself reflected as a South Asian Queer immigrant kid stuck in Central Connecticut. It was many years later where I met the brilliant Urvashi Vaid at a Creating Change conference, got my hands on a copy of Rakesh Ratti's "A Lotus of Another Color" (1993), Shyam Selvadurai's "Funny Boy" (1993) and Ruth Vanita's "Queering India: Same-Sex Love and Eroticism in Indian Culture and Society" (2001). While some circles know who these people are, there is just a deep gap in **our** story. As queer Desis, we are not just our ancestors' wildest dreams but we are the ancestors too. We are writing a collective history to ensure our journeys of queerness, brownness and all the overlapping aspects of our lives are witnessed, recorded, and celebrated. And adding our stories to the larger collective consciousness. Each of us has the ability and responsibility to take up space. This book is my offering towards our collective space-taking. Sharing stories is the oldest form of community building, coming from an oral history tradition that has preserved ancient texts, mythologies and philosophies for thousands of years. I hope this book is both read and spoken out loud. I want you to feel each word and sentiment embedded onto these pages. Everyone's story is worthy of such care which is why this is an interactive journey, connecting reader and author, you and me, into a collective "us." Even how we read a book makes it uniquely our own.

I imagine indigenous people all around the world looking at the night sky thousands of years ago and making meaning, identifying constellations out of what may seem like just a random sprinkling of stars across the Universe. From early Chinese and Egyptian cultures that mapped stars and formations to Greeks that developed constellations to celebrate heroes and mythologies, humans have tried to find ourselves in the night sky. What amazing vision and wisdom they had when staring at the stars, not too different from the ones we can see tonight, and finding patterns, creating stories and making sense of the chaos in galaxies far away! I believe we notice patterns and create constellations around us all the time. We make meaning from the world around us. I invite you to keep track of your reading journey by tracking *how* you read the memoir, because the journey is equally as important as the destination.

I've been asked "So, why a memoir?" and my answer, "Why not?" In "Old Friend from Far Away", Natalie Goldberg reminds us that *mémoire* in French refers to, "... the study of memory, structured on the meandering way we remember". It's not a life history or a retelling of a journey in a linear fashion to some grand "aha". It's a collection of stories, moments and memories. It's also not like social media where a filter-laden picture with a quippy tagline receives likes and comments. Memoir is somewhere in between, a place of joy, sadness, vulnerability and humanness. Little glimpses into a person's life built on a roller coaster as you journey together in and out of windows of time with lots of loops, turns and even unexpected obstacles. In this book, you are not merely a reader or passenger on this rollercoaster, you are a co-navigator extraordinaire! I call this an interactive memoir, one that requires the reader and author to break beyond the pages and sneak into each other's reality in between the words. Welcome to this journey!

May these memories spark your own remembrances. Our stories are now interconnected. We are "inter-are" as my teacher Thich Nhat Hanh says. I'm excited for this journey together as bookmates, like roommates but instead of sharing a physical space we will share the pages and words ahead. While all the stories in this book are true, I have taken some artistic license in using pseudonyms for certain people and changing contexts of certain stories to preserve anonymity where needed while maintaining the integrity of each piece.

This book is an offering. A prayer. A vision.
May our journeys honor our shared humanity, heal our past and build better worlds for all of us,
one story at a time.

Ways to Read this Book

As a kid, I loved the Choose-Your-Own-Adventure books where I became part of the storymaking by picking which chapter to read. A story is not just what's on a page but how it is read. I call this book an interactive memoir because I want you to have agency in how you understand the layers of this story, how you constellate meaning into the words and images. You can read the book in seemingly linear fashion from front to back as you would most books (though the chapters are not set up to follow a chronological order).

Or you can choose to close your eyes, take a deep breath and flip to a random page and start reading. See what comes up for you and continue this process after you read each piece. Make sure to track the order of the chapter number as you read so you can "connect the dots" in the Constellation Map. Start with this symbol (✪) in the middle of the page. With each connection you'll start to see the unique constellation you are creating, bridging the reader and author, you and me, creating a collective story. Your reading path makes it a unique story! If you are someone who likes to re-read books, you can try reading in a different order to see if the stories evolve differently or give you new insights!

Beyond reading, I have included several invitations and prompts where you can add your own story to this constellation, intertwining our stories further. Take time to reflect and write in the book or on a separate piece of paper. I want you to color the images within the book and even the cover, transforming this book into your own custom-made, one-of-a-kind edition! I urge you to share your writing and coloring with friends and on social media using the hashtag **#queeringconstellations**.

The Venerable Buddhist teacher, Thich Nhat Hanh says, "If you are a poet, you will see clearly that there is a cloud floating in this sheet of paper. Without a cloud, there will be no rain; without rain, the trees cannot grow; and without trees, we cannot make paper. The cloud is essential for the paper to exist. If the cloud is not here, the sheet of paper cannot be here either. So we can say that the cloud and the paper *inter-are*. 'Interbeing' is a word that is not in the dictionary yet, but if we combine the prefix 'inter-' with the verb 'to be,' we have a new verb, inter-be" (emphasis from the original text). Everything is connected and with this book, we are connected. And I hope you will share your art and writing, connecting with others who are sharing their work into our collective experience of this book. I can't wait to witness your space-taking journey.

Our interbeing is a critical notion in Buddhism, Hinduism and many other faiths where the entire world is seen as a balance of interconnectedness. Our stories and co-existence on this Earth means that each of our stories is a strand in a larger narrative of the Universe and somehow we all get woven, quite messily, into a collective fabric of human truth.

My story is no greater or lesser than yours. Our greatest resource is our story and our greatest barrier is our notion of what our story is supposed to be. Recognizing that time is both everlasting and yet limited is our greatest liberation. Our recognition that we may not have forever, but we have today. We have this moment. I get to breathe right now. And I don't even have to think about it! How will you read this book? What will you add from your own story?

How to Track Your Constellation of this Journey

As you read each letter, poem or story and color in each image, take a moment to identify the dot on the Constellation Map on Page ix. Draw a line to each dot as you complete a piece. You are welcome to skip any chapter/dot you'd like. There will be no book monitors checking to see if you haven't read or completed a section of the book! Over time you will start to see a new constellation evolve. Happy Constellating!

1 A NEW DAY WILL COME

My dear Sun hasn't stopped burning across the Sky each
morning,
My darling Moon hasn't stopped reflecting beams onto the
Earth each night.
So what cause do I have to worry about what tomorrow will
bring?

Tomorrow,
The Sun will rise
The Moon will shine
The Whales will meander
The Leaves will dance
The Trees will gather
The Snakes will shed
The Birds will soar
The Lovers will caress
The Healers will rejoice

The Music will soothe
The Spirits will guide
The Heart will heal
The Stars will gather

So what do I have to worry about what tomorrow will bring?
It will bring another chance to live, connect and be at peace
with myself and the Universe.

A new day will come.
As the Moon and Sun dance their Celestial tango
constellating stars into never-ending love letters
A new day will come.

2 SALIGRAMA - SHAPES OF LIFE

Black limestones, with more than 66 million years of meditation, flow down the Kali Gandaki River in Central Nepal to the various tributaries. While Ammonites are a common geological element found in every part of the world, these are special.

In the West, an Ammonite derives its name from Ammon, a fusion of the Greek deity Zeus and Egyptian god Amon-Ra, both sacred gods in their respective traditions.

I grew up knowing them as Saligramas - sacred manifestations of Vishnu. Each stone contains fossils and markings of ancient sea creatures, creating a coil that resembles Vishnu's Chakra, a wheel that has the power to destroy evil in this world. The Brits call them Snakestones for their resemblance to coiled snakes and share stories of Christian saints ridding communities of snakes by turning them into stones.

Snakes are sacred in many indigenous cultures, yet deemed to be the devil by Christians and are therefore vilified. I find snakes to be such deeply spiritual creatures and bridges within or across worlds and energies. From Egyptian royalty displaying images of snakes on their crowns to Hindu images of multiheaded snakes as protectors, ancient cultures have always honored the symbolism of these serpents.

My first introduction to snakes was when I was a kid. Often they took different roles based on the mythologies in which they exist. The Hindu god Vishnu is represented in his truest form as a blue-toned god sleeping on a thousand headed snake, Vasuki, who represents time in the midst of a milky ocean of the Universe. And Shiva lives in a cemetery and meditates in the Himalayas, wearing snakes as his jewelry. He even drinks the poison spewed when the Devas and Asuras decide to use the snake as a rope to churn the ocean, bringing life to all we know in this world, like churning butter from milk. And as a boy, Krishna wrestles then dances famously on Kalinga, a river serpent who is poisoning the river Yamuna. Subramanya is known as a manifestation of a divine snake and seen as a healer of the various energy centers, the chakras which lead to our spiritual evolution. And leave it to the Europeans to take from ancient Indo-Arabic cultures' understanding of these sacred cycles and forms and present it to the West, now known as the Fibonacci Sequence.

The mathematical equations and the spiral shapes of nautili, snakes, and *saligramas* serve as a reminder that life is not linear and has never been. In Hinduism, time is represented as a snake, clearly a beginning and an end, but not a line.

Swirling, intertwining, serpentine patterns capturing nature's desire for balance.

While time may be linear, life is anything but a line.

More likely a swirl, a spiral capturing creation going to eternity.

Why are we so obsessed with lines and linear ways of being? One Way. Straight forward, move on up the ladder.

Learning our lives are circular and spiraling is freeing. Because in a circle there is no beginning nor end. Spirals don't just go down, they also go up. Just being. Wherever you are, you have arrived. You are here. Unlike a line where we pass a particular point and it is gone, in a spiral or circle, we come back to these spaces time and time again, just with new knowledge, a different point of life and with more healing.

With each breath, each lifetime, we create new points of life, new shells, new skin, new constellations within our bodies.

Growth, renewal, evolution, revolution.

Life is anything but a line.

SPIRALS WITHIN ME

3 WE NEED THE DARKNESS

Why are we so ready to cast out the darkness?
Why are we afraid of the dark?

I come from darkness.
The depths of my Amma's womb, a galaxy of stars and cells
I come from darkness.
Melanin stitched into my spirit with ancestral threads and
treasures
I come from darkness.
Everything and nothing, all at once.

The depths of our eyes are black as the bridge between what
we see and what we feel. Darkness is the path and light
simply guides us.

I dream of worlds yet to be in the darkness of slumber.
I return to the darkness.

Releasing all the energy dragging me into the abyss of shame
I return to the darkness.
Ashes of death fluttering on the riverfront
I return to the darkness.
Everything and nothing, all at once.

Womb, Bridge. Death.

I am the Darkness, Light and Bridge.
We need the Darkness to free us from the Light. Releasing
this world around us and returning to the world within where
we not only envision freedom, we become it.

Darkness, Becoming, We need the darkness.

Why are we so ready to cast out the darkness?
Why are we afraid of the dark?

I come from darkness.
The depths of my Amma's womb, a galaxy of stars and cells
I come from darkness.
Melanin stitched into my spirit with ancestral threads and
treasures
I come from darkness.
Everything and nothing, all at once

The depths of our eyes are black as the bridge between what
we see and what we feel. Darkness is the path and light
simply guides us.

I dream of worlds yet to be in the darkness of slumber.
I return to the darkness.
Releasing all the energy dragging me into the abyss of shame
I return to the darkness.
Ashes of death fluttering on the riverfront
I return to the darkness.
Everything and nothing, all at once.

Womb, Bridge. Death.

I am the Darkness, Light and Bridge.
We need the Darkness to free us from the Light. Releasing
this world around us and returning to the world within where
we not only envision freedom, we become it.

Darkness, Becoming, Home.

4 CANYONS OF LOVE, OR WHY I KEEP VASELINE IN THE CABINET

My hands feel so small yet safe in hers. Amma's hand calluses feel like sandpaper against my five-year old fingers as we open the gate and enter the chaotic harmony of Fort Road. We just left my aunt's house and the temple right next to it - solid and functional even after several hundred years of being in the same spot. I smell Kaka's fruit stand before I see him batting off flies from all the ripe apples, oranges, sapotas, grapes and my favorite, mangoes. The sweetness of the mangoes overpowers all the others and I want to ask my mom for some mangoes, but I know better. We can't afford such luxuries. Before I dwell on this too much, the smell of fresh Tulasi garlands, sandalwood incense from the temple and automotive exhaust from the cars passing by engulf me and we are off! I can feel the grime-covered granite sidewalk under my bare feet that has held billions of footsteps, broken wrappers, fruit peels and memories that will remain mysteries for life.

We start walking with purpose, as if we are in a video game avoiding obstacles. I see old Christian nuns chanting rosaries and their white and blue robes clashing against their sapota colored skin. Just behind them, a dark-skinned, gray-bearded man whose eyes seem piercingly white against his dark eyeliner and bushy eyebrows. He carries an altar on his shoulders with a small brass lamp, bright marigolds and roses, silky peacock feathers and a framed photo of a goddess that I'm not familiar with but instinctively causes me to pray with my hands touching my heart. We see fancy white Ambassador cars that look like plump clouds with tinted windows whisk by as if none of this sidewalk dance matters to their world. We continue weaving in and out of school children in neatly pressed maroon uniforms and oiled braids with perfect ribbon bows. The big green military-grade bookbags on their backs holding at least twenty books and all the hopes and expectations of their families alongside beggars shaking beaten aluminum cups with a few coins to draw a little pity from the late afternoon shoppers and students. I see a skinny woman in a bright purple and green sari carelessly tucked into her hip with a yellow blouse that clearly doesn't go with this outfit, but her confidence makes it work since she's more focused on getting through the crowd while balancing a wide cream-colored wicker basket of vegetables on her head. It almost looks like an oversized crown for a beauty contest or as if she is imitating baby Krishna's father placing him in a basket and carrying him across the river to safety so he does not get killed by his evil uncle, Kamsa.

Amma yanks my arm and my brain jumps back to reality. We walk the next block past used shoe sellers on the footpath next to used book sellers, next to wall calendar sellers with every god, movie star and puppy you could imagine in bright neon colors and sparkly sequins. While we are walking past all this, I keep looking at the worn gold bangles clinking against my mom's pure dark chocolate skin, glistening like a freshly made candy bar in the sweet shop. We cross the seven-way intersection, past the wall covered in the smell of urine and old chewing tobacco spit. We're at the Raja Market - Avenue Road Bus Stand which is less a bus station and more of a mixture of vegetable sellers, ox carts, little yellow and black auto rickshaws beeping around us and old men that look exhausted and sweaty pulling carts overflowing with goods to be delivered. In all this chaos, a few big KSRTC red and yellow colored buses honked with conductors leaning off the bus, announcing their route as if they were auctioneers selling dreams and destinations. We quickly maneuver around a black and white cow that is slowly chewing on some banana leaves in the middle of the street without a care in the world for the chaos around it as the bell around its neck rings in sync as it chews on the street feast. We barely jump on the bus with my mom tugging my arm harder than usual to make sure I don't fall as the conductor's whistle and the driver's roaring of the engine sets us off on our journey home.

The bus isn't crowded, meaning there aren't people hanging off the doors but there are no seats and there are at least fifty people standing in the aisles. So we shuffle in the little space left behind the driver's seat and the backboard since this is the last bus and we have to get back so Amma can make dinner and check on my sister Manju to see if she's finished her homework and chores. Once the bus gets going on our one-hour ride to Yelahanka, I notice the metal floor of the bus is heating up from the motor below and it starts to feel like I'm standing on lava.

"Amma! My feet are burning. I can't stand it. Can we please just sit somewhere?"

"Where are your chappals? Did you leave them at Chiti's house again?! What am I gonna do with you?!"

"I'm sorry I forgot. I just want to sit!"

"Yeah, sure, let's just sit in our own private bus or car that your Appa left when he died." Sarcasm should've been my Amma's middle name.

"But it really hurts Amma."

"What do you want me to do about the bus, kanna? Ok, wear these."

She takes off her faded blue rubber sandals and shuffles them over to me. I wear them with gratitude for the relief and barrier against the metal lava. Yet I don't notice that now my Amma is clenching her jaws and trying to look forward as calmly as possible. The rest of the bus ride seems uneventful besides the constant screeching of the bus breaks and movement of people on and off the bus.

"Yelahanka! Last stop!" Finally our stop. We all jump off the bus like bees from a hive and I give Amma her chappals and we begin our walk home. I can see she's walking a bit slower than she was before the bus ride.

"*Amma, Einaythu?* What's wrong?"

"*Enu Illa, kanna. Saakagidhe.* Nothing, sweetheart. Just tired."

We get home and I start playing with my sister's toys while Amma makes dinner, feeds us and gets the kitchen cleaned up. Then as we bring out our sleeping mats and get settled into bed, I watch her sit on the Chapay (straw rug) for her nightly ritual, Vaseline. The calluses on her heels are the worst - from years of standing up for herself and protecting her children and sacrificing for others. The calluses look like canyons of earth, covered in dirt and dead skin. When I have touched them, they feel hard and soft at the same time. I can't imagine the stories embedded deeply in each crack of skin. Each a memory of touching the earth, each step a painful reminder of the journey she has taken and yet the hope for an easier journey for us. As the Vaseline glides across each canyon, there is a sigh of relief and pleasure. For a brief second, she gets to care for herself, like a warrior resting after a long day of battle, knowing there are more days and years of war ahead. And yet in this moment, as she looks at Manju and me (as I'm fake sleeping and watching her ritual), she smiles as a small tear runs down her left cheek, like a drop of rain on a drought-stricken land.

I never forgot my chappals anywhere from that day on, just in case we ended up having to stand behind the driver to get home.

Even now, decades later, everytime I put on shoes or stand on a bus, I think of Amma and this moment of unconditional love and sacrifice. And as I look at my feet with no calluses to be found, I'm grateful for the road she has walked that has led me to this life where I keep a small container of Vaseline in the cabinet, not out of necessity but of memory.

5 MOONKISSES

Dark skies and deep blue nothingness

How beautiful to know you are there even when I cannot see you. Hiding in plain sight, reminding me that you are not just the Moon in a perfect circle. In the darkness, you give way for the stars to shine. What a gift of humility. We need the darkness. You are emptiness.

Darkness becomes home.

A sliver of silver amidst the velvety night. The slightest light reflecting off an ashy ball seeking his lover, a bright ball too eager, yearning to catch sight of the slightest curve in the sky.

Reminds me of a lover's bashful smile. What a gift of love.

You are romantic.

Growing brighter by each night, reclaiming your rightful space and tracing your nightly rituals across the world. How are you always so consistent in your ever changing light? You are a gift of becoming.

The night sky is pierced as you bare more of yourself. Each shining ray of light reflecting each crater and boulder is an intimate conversation between us. Bearing witness to each corner and crevice, a gentle act of love. As you, my Moon, see me in all my craters and crevices.

Without shame,
without hiding.
You are a witness.

Slowly, slowly, slowly.
Each breath, an observation.
A mirror, an arc, a sickle
cutting through the rigid forest of masks built up to survive as a human on this Earth. Somehow the Moon finds me wherever I am.
I can feel her unpacking my soul's secrets and fears.
You are a seeker.

Each passing day is just a deeper yearning for the coming night. The darkness comforting me while my Moon starts to bathe me in light kisses. Each night becoming brighter, my Moon shining more light.

My Moonkisses more intimate.

It's as if the Goddess made you so bright to ensure that those in the darkness would be guided clearly. While the insecurities may lurk, making you question if your existence matters, lovers around the world look to you as a promise of their love. Not because of the Sun's reflection but for the ways you dance and calibrate your brightness and fullness and reveal a new you each night, keeping lovers yearning for more.

You are a lesson in transformation.

Neelamegha Shyama. Krishna with skin as deep as the heavy blue-gray rain cloud. A beautiful celestial melanin, making his eyes sparkle like the stars at night. And he comes from the sacred lineage of Chandra, the Moon.

My lover.

Because at night, in the darkness, the Gopis convene with Krishna in pure pleasure, maidens in love. And I yearn for the Moon that shines brightly, radiating off of Krishna's skin like a comet reflecting the holy obsidian. Will you join me so we can become sacred creatures dancing naked in the garden? Being divine.

Dusky skies reveal a long awaited sight. My windowsill is heavy with desire as I seek a sign in the sky. An ancient priest or lover decoding celestial perfection. At last, I spot my true love - vibrant, full, regal. I can almost feel the Moon's pride in being such a perfect circle in the sky. Have you ever witnessed such bliss? Is love even love if not professed under the spotlight of an attentive Moon?

A bitter sweet night - the Moon's fullness foreboding it's waning to come. Yet it is I that feels bittersweet. The Moon simply smiles back that all of life is as simple as a waxing and a waning, and the journey in between. Each night a personal Moonkiss, marking the ever changing Universe and celebrating our humanity - not always visible in full but always there for our embrace.

You are a lesson in acceptance.

Embracing the darkness each night, as a monthly reminder that our shadow sides are simply those that I have yet to heal but essential to all that makes me me. And such a humble act of community. We do not need to always sparkle to be enlightened. Embracing my darkness, I help the stars and constellations around me shine brighter in the night sky.

A sliver in the sky again. A crescent on Shiva's matted hair soothing his temper. A pearly crescent butterfly fluttering in the night sky. A reminder that being in process is itself a beauty to behold. A powerful journey, moving oceans and mountains, marking a delicate line in between yesterday and tomorrow while always living in today.

You are a lesson in patience.

Slowly, slowly, slowly.
Moonkisses
A cosmic salve healing all the bumps and bruises of our humanness, teaching us that perfection is a simple fleeting aspiration
and change, a simple fact of existence.

Each month, shedding skin, revealing wounds and wonders -

my beloved Moon shines by the Sun, sustaining this everlasting dance for my sake.
A celestial timekeeper.

You are a lesson in balance.

Whisper a little chant for me.
To what do we owe this monthly self-exploration?
Moonkisses, healing journeys upon the Earth.
Slowly, slowly, slowly.
You are my lesson in love.

MOONWISHES

6 READER'S POEM: THE MOON TOLD ME A SECRET TONIGHT

Dear Friend - This is your chance to write a poem. Whether you are a seasoned bard or a novice poet, I urge you to engage this prompt with an open heart.

Sit somewhere comfortable, with as few distractions as possible. I find I write best late at night, sitting on a couch with a cup of tea and instrumental background music. Or sit outside under the night sky and look up at the Universe. Look for the Moon in the sky. Do you see the Moon shining down brightly or as a shy sliver hiding amongst the Stars?
Take three deep breaths and feel the Moon coming out just for you.

Breathing In, Breathing Out - Relax your body
Breathing In, Breathing Out - Listen with your heart
Breathing In, Breathing Out - Open your eyes

What is the Moon speaking into your heart? Complete the prompt below with a poem. It could be a Japanese Haiku or long verse, whatever your heart desires. Enjoy!

THE MOON TOLD ME A SECRET TONIGHT

By:_____

8   SCARS AND BONDS

Dear Roji Akka -

Do you remember that night? These three amoeba-like marks on my waist are the oldest physical scars that I remember. I don't think about them often but every now and then I'll catch myself in the mirror after a shower and it makes me smile. Isn't it funny how such a painful memory can now elicit a smile? It's as if you're with me, Akka, with whose death I was given a life I never could have imagined. I don't remember exactly how old I was, probably around three or four and you were no more than seventeen, the oldest cousin in the family and the first grandchild.

No one except Thatha called you Rukmini, your given name. And you were his favorite; you preferred Roji for short because of your love of roja huvu (roses). Big brown eyes, long jet black hair neatly braided against your pale skin and the kumkum bottu on your forehead just made you look like a goddess. All the sisters were in town for some family celebration, and you were in the kitchen, talking with some of the aunties cooking and gossiping over the evening meal.

This house was over 200 years old and you had lived here until you got married a few years ago. We all hated the kitchen door, maybe five-feet tall; even shorter people in the family had to duck to enter and exit. I never understood why this particular door was so short when we also had eight-foot tall doors around the house. The kitchen door led into the main hall of the house, which then connected the other rooms. I loved this kitchen, and all the aromas that would come out of it every day. This kitchen was as big as the common room including high ceilings with a tiled roof, and even some skylights up top. Through the patches on the walls, I could see the generations of paint that held secrets of all the food that had been cooked, all the conversations that had been had, and all the family mysteries that had been covered up.

Moving in and out of this kitchen meant you had to go slow to make sure not to hit your head. And while the kitchen was relegated to the women, the main hall was relegated often to the men, both separated only by a five-foot tall door. Women were often only called when people needed beverages, food or needed someone to complain to. As an orthodox South Indian, Brahmin family, the patriarchy and gender roles were very clearly defined and enforced.

It was evening time, and I had been playing outside all day. I think you were asked by one of the aunts in the kitchen to take some hot water over to the other room for someone. I don't remember who it was for but drinking hot water is such a typical Indian thing to do, it could have been anyone. As the Sun disappeared into the horizon, I got home from playing with friends for most of the day.

I saw Paati, our grandmother, sitting in the front yard with her mortar and pestle clinking away at making some betel nut powder which she would put into betel leaves and chew. Isn't it funny how between this herbal concoction and her coffee about 10 times a day, this woman needed nothing else to live? You know, in the U.S., people drink grandes, ventis and other absurd sizes. Paati, you and everyone in India at that time would drink little steel cups of very milky and sugary coffee that were maybe a little larger than an espresso cup. You remember how Paati could be sleeping, and if someone mentioned coffee she would immediately wake up!? It was also common practice for her to call any grandkid around to go ask one of the women in the kitchen to make some coffee for her. She wasn't a big fan of me (I think she partially blamed me for her son's death, my father, because she saw me as a bad omen since he died after I was born. But that's like blaming the Sun for a car accident that happened right after it dawned). But I was still good enough to be her messenger/coffee servant. "Hogi solpa kapi thogundbaro." "Go get me some coffee." she said. In my never ending attempt to redeem myself for my birth, I glee-fully agreed and started running through the house towards the kitchen.

I have memories of you recounting the story as you remember it: you picked up a steel cup full of hot water, which then made the cup itself difficult to hold so you held it with your finger *tips and started walking towards the common room. At this exact moment, I turned the corner towards the kitchen entrance. Crash.*

All I remember is hearing the sound of the stainless steel cup falling against the cement floor, like an alarm going off without a snooze button. As my consciousness comes back to me, I realize I'm on the floor face down, with tears running down my face, but my mouth seems to be unable to make any sounds from the pain. I notice you standing there, frightened with an expression that looks like you've just seen a ghost. All the women in the kitchen rush towards me. "Ayyo! Yeanaithamma?! Ella seriyohgathe bidu." "Oh goodness! What happened, little one? Everything is gonna be ok."

And then I start to feel my body burning with pain. I look over my right shoulder and I see bubbles from where the hot liquid had touched my waist. It's like I'm being burned alive, but the adrenaline is still coursing through my body so I'm still unable to speak and in shock. By now, a crowd of all the family has gathered and you are a mess, crying uncontrollably. Kanna Chitha comes rushing through the crowd to see what's going on, immediately picks me up, puts me on his shoulder and starts carrying me through the house, saying, "It's OK chinna, you're gonna be fine. We're going to the hospital." As I feel myself coming back into my body, I notice my Amma just behind us, followed by you, and the rest of the family as we parade down the road to the little neighborhood doctor's medical clinic, like we're all making a family pilgrimage. I can still hear you sobbing, "I'm so sorry, I'm so sorry!" as we get to the clinic. It's where we go for everything - a local Doctor who has been the doctor to the community for decades - we only go to hospitals for "major things". Guess second degree burns weren't major enough.

The doctor was kind, calmed me down, examined my burns, prescribed some ointment and sent us on our way. On the way back, Chitha stopped us at the little corner store and bought me the largest Cadbury chocolate bar he could find and my own bottle of Maaza (the most delicious mango drink!) which did make me happier! I notice you just lagging behind and being comforted by Amma and some of the other aunties.

The pain was terrible, and the next few days were miserable. I could not go out to play with my friends. My skin was still peeling, and I was grouchy. I was only able to lay on one side without being able to move. You never entered the room. You would always just stand outside and watch. You would bring me lunch but then give it to Amma to feed me. As the kid in the family who had learned to be quiet and invisible, this was a strange experience. I felt bad about yelling at you that night, but I wasn't sure how to apologize yet and so we just exchanged silent eye conversations for the whole week. Everyone else kept coming in and out to check on me. It was fun to be the center of attention for once but also really uncomfortable. I loved the chocolates and toys that I got, but I hated the pity in everyone's face as they looked at me.

Thankfully, the burns got better, and I could go back to being invisible around the house. And I remember you bathing me once during Deepavali and you started sobbing once you saw the scars. "It's ok Akka, it doesn't hurt anymore and I know it was just an accident." I say as I wipe tears from your face, "I should have been slower to turn the corner. Don't cry Akka. I don't like when you cry."

A few years later, you died just after childbirth due to a stupid brain hemorrhage that devastated the entire family. You were always sweet and loved by everyone, the perfect child. Your Appa and Amma, my aunt and uncle, were living in the U.S. and as soon as they heard, they flew back to India. They were heartbroken, and in many ways have never recovered from losing you. Their goal was always to get settled in the U.S. and then sponsor you and your family to move to the U.S. with them. Your death shattered so much of their spirits.

After the traditional thirteen days of funeral rites, your Appa and Amma spoke to my Amma and asked if they could adopt me and bring me to the U.S. They were suffering and wanted a child of their own and to lessen Amma's burden of being a widow in India with many children to care for. I can't imagine that this was an easy conversation for either party. How does one ask for another's child when you're still grieving your own? How does one agree to give a child to someone else to live in a land far away? So many complicated life decisions at such young ages. I did not know then but now I'm able to appreciate the amount of bravery required by my aunt and uncle (soon to become my Mummy and Daddy) and my Amma (soon to become a stranger to me) to enter into this family contract. It all happened so quickly. Within six months of your death, I arrived in a strange land called New York City in the middle of March.

And here we are thirty-five years later. As I have grown, the scars on my waist have grown as well. They're paler now, but they are still there. I like to think that the Universe was bridging our lives together, a foreshadowing of a life that could have been yours, and has become my pathway to self-aware-ness and healing.

But your shoes are still too big for me to fill. At some point, I stopped trying to be the perfect child, like you. A few years ago, I had a therapist tell me, "You know, you can try all you want but you'll never be as good as their dead child, since she can't do any wrong. It's better you learn to be yourself rather than trying to be a perfect substitute for a perfect dead daughter."

I don't love all the scars on my body, but these... these, I love so much. Every time I think of you, I touch my scars and I can feel your presence. I know you have been one of my guardian angels in so many different situations in my life, every time I've needed you, you've been there. Thank you for being there for me and for gifting me this life. You know, now I love drinking hot water. But I make sure to use large, insulated mugs, preferably with lids given how clumsy I am.

Love and gratitude -

Raja

9 WE ARE THE SALVE, WE ARE THE HEALING

Today, I listened to an artist speak about coming out to his
mother about his HIV status, and how she said,
"I am here and I hold you
and I will always be here, my sweet child.
We will figure it out together."

And I cried for my mother.
I cried to know her.
To feel her touch on my head,
to feel her hands strengthen my spine,
making me stronger, making me a little bit taller.
Releasing this weight of shame that I hold around me.

Who is this stranger? This mother of mine. A woman whose
truth is wrapped up in a sari so tightly that it suffocates any
light or spirit.

Today, I saw a film that spoke about a mother's love,
accepting her gender nonconforming child. Though she did
not have all the information, she recognized the strength of
the child and the struggle they had gone through until this
point, holding a secret that felt like a world crashing on one's
spine.

The mother says,
"You have always been my child,
and you will continue to be my child,
and I love you not in spite of who you are.
Because of who you are."

I feel tears
rolling down my cheeks
like raindrops against the window pane slowly following
uncharted pathways,
meandering
down
towards
my
heart.

Each tear,
full of moisture
and melancholy.

Each drop wet and cold
against
my warm and angry skin.

With each heartbeat, the temperature of my skin becomes
like tea
boiling
on the stove.

The water at my eye's edge blurs my vision,
making me question if what I am seeing is
reality or simply desire.

A vision.
For a mother that had the capacity to be there for me
For a mother who can show emotion beyond sadness and fear
For a mother, who resides in my spirit, even on my darkest
days and in my lowest valleys
A mother who is intertwined into my pain and liberation.

Today, I read Thay's reminder to
imagine my mother as
a five year old child.
What does the five year old child in you desire?
What is your vision for your life?
What do you need to feel healed?
What do you need to feel at peace?

Or simply what do you need to feel?

Today, I cried for myself. For a childhood that was stripped
away too quickly, for parents who were in so much pain that
they could not care for me in the way that I needed.
For my family who have carried so much generational trauma

and live in superficial relations with each other in fear of
conflict.

Dear Prakruthi - Mother, Goddess of Creation
This is my prayer:
Let me become the seed of healing within myself.
Let each of us become
our own salve,
our own healing,
in community.

Plant your divine wisdom and compassion in each seed.
Plant the divine gem found in the heart of the lotus into each
of us.

May my mother guide me in building
a spiritual womb, a secret bond,
a divine and unshakable sense of belief and purpose, to
guide me
in
my true purpose.

May my love for her become a true manifestation of my truth.
May
she
forgive
herself.
And those around her.

May the divine Mother embrace her children,

May we all hold tightly the divine that
lives within us
and share the light,
transformative in all the beautiful ways possible.

Om, Shanti, Shanti, Shantihi

10 FURY FOR A PURI

Amma, Akka and I lived in a small room at the back of the family house at 200 Bhestara Bhidi. The room was small, probably 10 x 7 feet or so, just big enough for our sleeping mats and Amma's trunk which held anything of value we had in life. The trunk included Appa's photo, her few saris, Akka's and my school uniforms, report cards and whatever dignity my mother had left after years of being seen as a bad omen because she became a widow at twenty-one.

In front of the house was a triangular courtyard of dirt which served as a hang out for adults, a playground for all the cousins and where my cousin Roji's body was laid for family visitation when she died.

Directly across the street was a small restaurant with a metal rollup door and a couple of chairs that went out front. It was an Udupi restaurant, which was run by an orthodox family from the Western coast of Karnataka that lived upstairs and had the most delicious and steaming idlis and sambar, bisi-belebath and my favorite - puri and saagu. Puri is a deep fried, flat wheat bread and saagu is a yummy dish of potatoes, peas and lots of spices in an aromatic gravy of cilantro and chilies, all served on a banana leaf. At five years old, it was the closest thing I knew to heaven.

Just by walking out the front door, I could smell the various spices searching for my nose and making my tummy grumble. The chef and owner was a tall, lanky, pale skinned man in his 30s with jet black hair, and matching mustache with nothing but a white cotton panche (dhoti/robe) wrapped around his waist. I had only eaten at the restaurant a handful of times in my whole life. Having a joint family with a house full of women meant our kitchen was operating at all times of the day. The women in the family cooked such delicious, aromatic food that I never really needed other food and yet the smells and flavors from the restaurant always flirted with me in the worst way possible. Especially on weekends, I would ask Amma if I could just get some puri from the restaurant and invariably every time the answer was, "And what are we supposed to do with all this food in the kitchen? You think your Appa left a fortune for me to get you hotel food every-day? Just eat whatever prasadam we made for the temple and stop bugging me. There's so much work to be done." You see, being a widow in our family meant that, while my father had passed away, she was still expected to live with his family in a large house altogether, with very little privacy, or more impor-tantly, very little agency in her life. Besides taking care of my sister and myself, Amma became a de facto maid in the family, getting up at three o'clock in the morning everyday so she could start the fire under the aunde - a big metal water tank built into cement with a small opening below for wood, coconut shell scraps and other burnables, ensuring that the water would be hot and ready for everyone's shower in the morning. Even though now the house has an electric water heater, she still gets up an hour before everyone else to turn it on, so it's ready for their use.

Amma had stopped going to school after tenth grade because her parents said "that's enough education for a girl and to make a good wife". As a young widow, she had the bad luck of being in a family where women working outside the house, or having their own income, was not allowed, and even frowned upon. Without a husband, Amma was at the mercy of her in-laws, who were not the nicest people in the world. The room that they gave Amma, Manju and I was literally next to the room that held the family's cows, the well, and the laun-dry/dishwashing station, which really just was a large piece of granite used as the washboard next to a couple of barrels of water and a little opening in the wall that took the dirty water to the street sewage canals.

I honestly don't know how she was able to care for both my sister and I and make sure that we had books, uniforms and tuition money. My Appa was the second of eight brothers and three sisters (my Patti had given birth to other children but these were the ones that made it to adulthood) and of these, my favorite was Kanna Uncle. He was the fifth brother and had a room to himself in the older part of the house, just a few rooms down from our shack. He was single and unlike all the other brothers, he was not a priest, rather he worked at the post office in Bengaluru about 30 kilometers away. While my sister was more social with the other cousins and family members, I was quite shy and mischievous. But with Kanna Uncle I felt like I could be myself. He would help me with homework every day after he came home from work and I would often sleep next to him in the comfy bed rather than having to squeeze next to Amma and Manju on the floor in our little room. He would speak to me in English every morning, making sure I did my morning yoga exercises, and said my prayers as soon as I woke up and before I went to bed. To this day, he is the only uncle that I actually call "uncle", everyone else is just "chitha" which means younger uncle in Tamil. I found out years later that he also helped my Amma with school fees so I could attend the English medium school rather than the public Kannada based school. Though India had been an independent country for almost 40 years, the desire for Anglo culture and English as a sign of prestige, access, and intelligence was deeply rooted at all levels of society, including the popularity of English based schools that were seen as being better than schools teaching in local native languages.

My favorite part of the day with Kanna Uncle was our morning beverage ritual. He kept a special stash of Ovaltine in his dresser just for me. Along with a cute little ceramic cup and saucer set, every morning he would make sure my mother would make the Ovaltine and he would serve it to me, so that we could have the special ritual before I went to school and he went off to work. Having never known my father, Kanna

Uncle was both the fun uncle and an additional parental figure that I needed in my earlier years. Whenever I needed to feel safe or got into an argument with my Akka or my Amma, I would hide under his bed and wait until he came home to give me a hug and advocate on my behalf, or just get me a piece of Cadbury's chocolate to make me feel better. Even after he got married, he made sure our morning rituals continued. His wife knew that in marrying him, I was part of the package.

I was not so lucky with my other uncles, especially Murali Chitha. He is younger to Kanna Uncle and as long as I've known him, he's always been grumpy, always chewing on some Pan Parag while yelling obscenities at anyone that happens to cross his path. I had learned to stay away from him, but this one Sunday our fates were intertwined. Sunday, being a school holiday, I had finished my bath and recited all my prayers, and was going to walk over to a friend's house to play. Even before I reached the front door to step outside, I could smell the aromas of fluffy idlis and crisp puris teasing my hungry stomach from the restaurant across the street. I stepped outside with a smile on my face. In the dirt court-yard, I saw Murali Chitha sitting on a plastic chair with a large metal plate covered with at least a dozen puris and a bowl of steamy saagu.

"Hey Chitha!"

"Ugh. What do you want?"

"What are you up to?

"Are you blind? Can't you see I'm trying to enjoy my Sunday breakfast?"

I should have just walked away and then it would've been a Sunday like any other, but no. My stupid ass self was hungry and I said, "It looks yummy. Can I have a bit of puri? "

"No. This is my food. I'm not your goddamn father."

That hit a sore spot. My father, his older brother, was not around because he was dead. I wasn't asking him to be my father. As a family where my grandparents, all six uncles and their families (since the eldest already resided in the US)) all lived in one multi-generational and dysfunctional house, I had assumed a simple request for a bite was not a big deal. I was five years old for goodness sake. I was so furious, more about his words than the food, but I wanted to teach him a lesson.

So I lunged forward, almost like a lion going after its prey and clawed a piece of puri from his plate, stuffing it into my mouth. His eyes got big and red as he leapt up out of the chair and threw the plate against the wall as if it was a frisbee and the wall was a dog. The steel plate hit the wall with a loud bang and food flew everywhere! This is all in a matter of seconds, but it felt like I was watching a slow motion movie that I couldn't escape.

I was in shock and I didn't know what to do, but I knew I couldn't stand there. So I took two steps back slowly, pivoted toward the house door and ran for my life. Down the corridor, past stairs that go up to my Thatha's room and into the great hall. I could hear him screaming profanities not far behind me. His right hand raised in a fist above his head, still with food dangling from the fingertips. *"Kahthe nun magane, naanivathu ninna saayisabiduthene"* "Son of an ass, I'm gonna make sure to murder you today!"

I stare at all the pictures on the wall, as if I'm stopping to ask for directions on how to save my life. Not getting any answers, I look back and notice him picking up a machete that was tucked in the corner of the entryway. A tool usually used for husking coconuts was about to become the tool for my beheading. I run straight into the kitchen to see if I can find my mom (making sure to not hit my head on the doorway), but not seeing her, I exit the back of the kitchen towards the bathroom around the corner past the aunde that still has some embers burning bright underneath, and then almost trip on the threshold as I enter the other common room. There are a few aunties and grandmothers prepping some vegetables for a festival meal the next day as they sit on straw mats on the ground and gossip away. In my family, anyone old enough to be your Amma is called an aunty, and anyone older immediately becomes Paati, grandmother. I still am not sure how most people are related to me in my extended family, but I have dozens of aunties and Paatis. I jump over the large granite, mortar and pestle, built into the ground and quickly land right next to one of the Paatis, trying to catch my breath.

"Yaen aithu, kandha?" "What happened, dear?" She asks. But before I could respond, I heard him yelling "I'm coming for you!!!" I leap like an impala avoiding the lion and almost slip on the straw mat, but I jump over the vegetables and quickly

rush into Kanna Uncle's room and sneak under the bed. This Paati came behind me and closed the door, making herself a human shield of steel between the raging monster with a machete and me.

Through the closed door, I hear him yelling and the aunties and Paatis trying to reason with him. "He's just a kid! Calm down!" He's still steaming but now I hear my Amma's voice. She had come out of nowhere! She's already sobbing - a mix of sadness and anger as she confronts Murali Chitha.

"Yaen aithu?"

"Your child destroyed my meal. I was just eating and he stole my puri."

"So now you want to kill him? Go ahead. While you're at it, why don't you kill me too and you can sell our organs for all the puris you want." My Amma had a great flair for the dramatic. But I've learned over the years that her dramatic responses are more out of necessity for survival than desire for drama.

Now Amma turns to Paati, "Let me at him. I'm going to give him such a beating, he won't ever want a puri in his life!"

Paati, my guardian angel that day, starts talking as if she's a judge over a trial, "Everyone calm down. No one needs to be sacrificed today. Here, give me the machete," she gestures to the monster, "Come to the kitchen and I'll make you some coffee." The other aunties joined in their pleas.

By now I was peeking through a crack in the door at the whole debacle. He was still steaming but after a few minutes, he put down the weapon and headed to the kitchen. While I was relieved that he was gone, now I was more worried about my fate. Amma was sitting with some of the women crying and beating her palm on her head.

"I'm going to kill this kid or he'll give me a heart attack! Why is he such a pain?! Why can't he just stay out of trouble?! Maybe his father was right. My life would be so much easier without worrying about him all the time. Why can't he be like Manju?!"

The door stays locked and the Paati stands guard until Kanna Uncle comes home and hears the entire drama as he opens the door. I'm sitting on the bed, dried tears and snot covering my face and arms. Amma is just outside the door making threats, "*Ninna charrma sulidhubidutene, nodthairu.*" "I'm going to skin you alive, just you wait." which is her poetic way of saying you're going to get a beating you won't forget. Kanna Uncle enters, doesn't say a word and just hugs me. I start crying and snotting again.

For me it was about just wanting a puri. For my Amma it was about pride. Having her child begging or stealing food from others, especially from family members who did not hide their disdain for us living there, was a reminder of not being able to provide for her children. Such a problem would not exist had her husband still been alive. It was another reminder of this delicate prison she navigated, putting up with her dead husband's family, while feeling the weight of raising children who would not be dependent on others or be seen as charity cases. Seeing her cry while she was beating the shit out of me made me cry from physical pain and a deep guilt for causing her such anguish.

I don't remember what time I fell asleep that day, covered in bruises. Let's just say the beating was so effective that I still don't like puris and will opt for chapatis, naan or rice when given the chance.

11 INSTRUCTIONS INCLUDED: HOW TO LOVE ME

Even on the hardest days,
Love me.
It's worth the effort.

I was taught there is no time for love.
Love was presented as a scary word worthy of fear.
Now I know those fears were foolish.
Why be afraid of the divine?
A prayer of pleasure.

Kiss me. Breath life to my dreams and scaffold my heart,
reaching for my aspirations.

Touch me. Each touch of your fingers across my skin
A silent ballad, skin to skin, heartbeat to heartbeat, melanin to
melanin

Let your fingers get lost in the maps of scars across the sandal-wood terrain of my skin

Soothe me. Let me crumble into your arms, weary from years of burden and pain.

Nourish me. I don't just mean with food, though I do love a good meal. Swirl your world with mine as we create never before seen intricacies and desires

Lick me. Let me feel the warmth of your tongue devour all of me. I want your spit and my sweat to know each other like childhood friends who know all of each others' secrets

Breathe me in. Savor the divine delicacy of my day-old musky sweetness, wafts of fresh orange blossoms, spicy curry powder, soft saffron petals, and just a little touch of the salty ocean breeze.

Dream with me.
Let us build towers of hope and playgrounds of pleasure.
Pools of rosewater and orchards of freedom.

Love me with your voice.
Each word, an ocean of sweetness, gets me hard and horny.
Tell me tales of queens and forbidden love.
Teach me words that make you giggle
and sounds that make your toes curl with gratification.

Pray with me. Pray for us. Pray for the journeys that have
brought us together and the stars that stitch our fates together.
We are not those star-crossed lovers; we are star-stitched
lovers. Each one becoming a prayer simply because
we choose
a pleasureful love against all odds.

What god is greater than love?
What prayer is stronger than a breath?
What purpose is greater than a lover's touch?
What need is stronger than my heart's desire?
What time is greater than now?
Love me in gentle looks across the yard
Love me with inside jokes that only we find funny
Love me by loving all of yourself
Love me in wanting a better tomorrow, not just for us, but for
our communities
Love me with little surprise notes in my bag
Love me with sweet kisses down my back
Love me by showering me with your jizz so it can dry
amongst my hair and remind me of what we did three times
on the kitchen floor last night.

I want a thunderous love, unafraid of the world we live in
and spreading me open as a gleeful tingle goes down my back

Like shooting stars sparkling across the night sky
and like the ocean reflecting on ocean's skin,
wet with desire.

Love me by being yourself
I am no saint and I need no penance
I am flesh and fire
A prayer of pleasure

12 A PINK BUNNY AND A PRINCESS: THE MAKING OF A BABY QUEER

March 1990. I set foot in the U.S. dressed in my three piece gray suit that's just a bit too small on my growing frame as Gorbachev becomes president of the Soviet Congress and Janet Jackson wins three Soul Train Music Awards. My Periya and Periamma (older uncle and aunt soon to be called Daddy and Mummy) pick me up in New York City and we make the twenty-one hour ride in a coach-class Amtrak train. I only remember it being a long trip and staring at lots and lots of farms out the window.

Home is now Lemont, IL, population: 7,875 people including the three of us. We live at the edge of the temple complex in an old two-story house shared with Ramu, a distant cousin and his parents. Ramu is just a few months older than me but makes it clear from day one that he and I are *not* the same. Having been in the U.S. for about two years already, his pale skin, "American" accent and American (read white midwestern) friends, he says I'm not allowed near his toys and while we may live together, we are not to acknowledge this fact to anyone at school.

In Yelahanka, I was thriving in second standard (grade) at Bharat English School, a private english-medium campus with my sister, cousins and other students who were Hindus, Christians, and Muslims and came in a spectrum of skin tones from white clouds to dark coffee. My best friend, Bhanu, was a Malayalee Christian boy and the palest kid I knew (like the color of a cup of milk with a few drops of coffee). I was a shy kid but when I was with Bhanu and my cousins, mischief surely followed. We attended tuition (tutoring sessions) each evening after school and even most Saturdays. I liked school but hadn't enjoyed all the times I had been told to stand on a bench and be smacked with a switch for a wrong answer or just some innocent whispering at the back of the class.

First day of school. In Lemont, I began in second grade (same class as Ramu, go figure) and was totally lost. A new home, a new family, and a new country might do that. Though English was my fourth language, my inability to keep up with class material meant the teacher decided I was not ready and therefore placed me in Mrs. Egg's first/second-grade hybrid class as a first-grader. Ramu made fun of me for weeks, but I quickly settled in and appreciated the review of material I had learned in India as I got into a new rhythm. I couldn't make any friends and Ramu telling everyone at school that I was demoted because I was stupid didn't help.

Easter wasn't anything interesting to me since I wasn't Christian and couldn't figure out who this Jesus guy was and why he liked bunnies, eggs and candy. That Fall, I was to continue in Mrs. Egg's class for second grade. She was the coolest teacher who helped me not feel stupid for asking questions and gave us time to nap every day! We never got those in India! In mid-October, she announced that we would be having a Halloween parade and party at the school. All kids were to come in costume and bring a treat to share.

"Excuse me, Mrs. Egg. What's Halloween?"

The class laughs.

"Calm down class. That's a great question Rajagopal. Does anyone want to answer?"

"It's where we get into fun and scary costumes and go get candy from all the neighbors!" said one of the kids.

"That's great, Tina! It's a celebration of the Fall season and yes, children put on different costumes and go trick-or-treating."

"Oh ok. I don't know if we celebrate that," I say, never having heard of Halloween among the dozens of Hindu festivals we celebrated in our family.

At home, I ask Mummy, "Do we celebrate Halloween? My teacher said we have to put on a costume and bring treats."

"Well, I don't think we do," she says as she rubs her fingers against her temples, "But let's ask Ramu and his mom to see what they do."

Ramu's mom says it's some wacky American holiday where children become ghosts and superheroes but because we are "good" Hindus, we don't celebrate such foolishness.

"But can I just be Batman or Big Bird or something, Mummy?"

"No, we're not spending money on this thing," she says as she's trying to get dinner ready. "We'll just put a panche on you and you can pretend you are Gandhi!"

I roll my eyes and accept defeat. I'm sad, but I tell Mrs. Egg that we're not Christian so we don't celebrate it. "Oh come on, you're in America and this is an American holiday. I'll bring some of my daughter's old costumes so you won't be the only kid left out of the parade." Halloween is on a Wednesday so that morning I get super excited for school and even get ready before Mummy yells at me. I get to school and see a box at the front of the room. Mrs. Egg asks me to pick out one of the outfits that might fit. Police officer or pink bunny. Obviously, my queer little heart leapt at the sight of the cutest pink bunny outfit in the world (yes, it was the *only* pink bunny outfit I had seen in my life but still). I put it on over my clothes and stayed a bunny the entire school day, through the parade, through lunch, through recess and through a math lesson. By the end of the day, I felt like I had become the pink bunny. Even more than all the chocolates, cupcakes and veggie sticks we got to eat, I was mesmerized with this costume. It made me feel different, like I was me but also a different person. Like I was special. I didn't want to take it off but with a sullen face, I started to become human again.

"Hey kiddo, why don't you keep the outfit for the day," the teacher says, seeing how sad I am. "This is your first Halloween! How exciting! You know, my neighbor does a great haunted house and my daughter is going trick-or-treating in the neighborhood. Why don't you ask your parents if it's ok to come over? We can pick you up around 4:30."

I didn't really know what a "haunted house" was but I didn't care since I'd get to wear the costume longer! I somehow was able to convince my parents to let me go and the next thing I know, I'm walking with Ellie, Mrs. Egg's daughter and her friends through the neighborhood with a plastic shopping bag in hand and a flashlight in the other and the biggest smile ever across my face. M&Ms, KitKats, Snickers, Jolly Ranchers, Big Reds, I just couldn't believe I was getting to eat all the candy I had seen on T.V. in India! America is awesome. With a stomach full of candy, we got to the Haunted House that looked pretty scary. "I'm not sure I wanna go there," I say. Ellie assures me it's not too scary but if at any time I want to leave we can. She was dressed as a princess so I figured I was safe. No one's gonna mess with a princess, even in a haunted house. She held my hand through the entire house. It wasn't that scary, just a bunch of teens in masks. We walked back to her house and Mrs. Egg and Ellie drove me home with my bag full of candy. Even though I had to leave the costume at their house, I was the happiest kid in the world that night as I slipped into bed.

There used to be a picture of me in my pink bunny outfit but it's been lost over time and our many moves. However the memory of that magical night is clear as day for me. Being the pink bunny was the beginning of my exploration of queerness and costumes. I spent the next few Halloweens as a police officer, Gandhi, and a prince. By the time I was in middle school, I convinced my parents to buy me a Caveman outfit (a leopard print polyester dress with some black felt that went over one shoulder and ended above the knees) so that I could repurpose it for Bharatanatyam performances as Shiva, the Hindu god of dance and someone who is often portrayed wearing animal skin attire. But the freezing Connecticut halloween night was too much to be walking around in the thinnest Shiva costume. The next year, I didn't have any money so I convinced my mom to let me wear her rainbow colored salwaar kameez which she rarely wore but kept in her closet. For hair I used a long black wool hooded scarf made into a braid with some strategic rubber bands and bejeweled with my dance jewelry. Mummy even let me wear some of her bangles and lipstick! It was definitely warmer than the caveman getup, and I felt much prettier and loved cat-walking down the neighborhood. For once I felt like I was pretty. I usually trick-or-treated alone and this year was no different. Not too long into trick or treating, some jerks started bullying me yelling "fag" and "sissy", following me from house to house. There was one house in the neighbor-hood that always had a Haunted House so I ran in and imag-ined Princess Ellie holding my hands. I felt better as I snuck in a corner until the boys came through. I jumped out from behind the mummy and they almost peed their pants and started running away. I couldn't stop laughing. Raja could have never done that. Being a princess gave me the courage to stand up for myself.

I was a theater kid and a dancer starting in elementary school but it wasn't until my first Halloween Princess that I realized how much I enjoyed playing with gender and feeling pretty. I secretly stashed the black scarf at the bottom of my closet so I could wear it late at night when everyone else was asleep and pretend I was a princess, like Rapenzel looking out the window waiting for her prince but ready to beat up some neighborhood bullies if needed. Mummy caught me dancing in the middle of the night as I was fully decked out in her clothes, make-up and hooded scarf braid. "Boys don't do this," she said as she made me promise not to do it again and closed the door. I would play dress up regularly, allowing the Princess to take over, replacing a shy, nerdy, skinny Brown kid with no friends with a confident, powerful and beloved leader of an imaginary world that spread as far as my imagination took me. I will forever be grateful to the Pink Bunny and the Princess for giving me the courage to be myself, transforming the nerdy shy kid into a confident baby queer to today's proud Brown gender-fluid being.

13 GENDER CHAMELEON: PRONOUNS AND THE PERFORMANCE OF GENDER

"Why do you have to make it so difficult for me? "
"You know my 9th grade teacher told me that 'they' is not singular? It's just not good English."
"What's wrong with you?"

This is my daily life. These comments come from friends and strangers alike. I began using gender inclusive pronouns of *they/them/theirs* in 2015 yet today, in 2025, I'm still misgendered regularly and told "But you don't *look* transgender!" and "It's just too hard to get used to this pronoun thing." Even people who lead diversity work have repeatedly misgendered me. I can't begin to tell you the personal anxiety caused from the newest version of my imposter syndrome: not being "gender queer enough".

So why are pronouns important?

Beyond one's name, a pronoun in most languages is the most important indicator of one's gender. Gender inclusive singular pronouns have been part of the English language for many centuries. Many authors, even as far back as the fourteenth century have used singular gender inclusive pronouns in their works and in non-Western traditions, even longer. I use the term "gender inclusive" rather than "gender neutral" because my intention is not to neutralize gender but to expand and complicate it.

I am, and always have been a gender rebel, one who refuses to let the strandard binaries of gender impact who I am and more importantly how I choose to express myself. From fighting with my parents to let me learn the Indian classical dance form Bharatanatyam to wearing a three piece tuxedo to prom or donning three-inch wedges to my doctoral graduation, I have always felt most like myself when I am blurring external expectations of who I am and how I'm supposed to show up. And yet, such rebellion comes at a cost. I can't begin to tell you the number of nights I have spent overthinking interactions with friends and family, trying to understand if something I did or said that day made me 'not enough'. Though misgendering me seems unconscious to them, I can assure you I notice it. And sometimes I'm just too exhausted to say anything. This is my self-preservation. As someone with multiple intersectional and historically marginalized identities, I'm used to many forms of internalized "-ism's" showing up and that makes it even more complicated. Trying to figure out which marginalized, or even dominant aspect of my identity is causing this self-doubt and sleepless nights is exhausting.

Pronouns, like names, are important indicators of who we are. When I first began using *they/them*, I did it as an act of advocacy for my students. I was working in an LGBTQ campus resource center and saw that many of my trans and gender queer students were having to face continuous experiences of being misgendered and misnamed, especially by faculty and university administrators. I figured if I could use both masculine (he/him) and gender inclusive (they/them) pronouns, my peers and campus leaders could practice using these unfamiliar pronouns while also being able to give some grace if they screw up. In doing so, I unexpectedly saw that I felt more comfortable expanding my gender expression by wearing nail polish, long earrings and even dressing in more culturally feminine ways; things I have always done in my own home or with friends but never at work. Even as the director of a center focused on sexual and gender diversity, I had not realized how, as Kenji Yoshino would put it, I was "covering" my gender for most of my life. I remember years of hiding my gender queerness by intentionally removing these identifiers in parking lots and bathrooms before going to work or family events to uphold my own internalized binaries of gender and not wanting to "cause a scene" or be "unprofessional".

As I began to broaden my gender presentation, I felt more in my skin and decided to use they/them full-time. I gave quite a bit of grace to my peers and folks that misgendered me because I know change is hard but when people would continue to use he/him only, even when I'm in the room and after repeated correction, it was painful. At first I tried to ignore it and felt silly for feeling such shame and pain for someone else's misstep but then realized it's because such misgendering brought up my own insecurities and I should not have to apologize for someone else's inability to see my gender queerness. I even had a friend say, "If only you wore long earrings or something all the time, it would help me remember." That one hurt. Requiring me to meet some invisible standard of gender-bending was still asking me to accommodate an external source for my own validation. Some days, I don't want to wear long earrings or heels. And that's ok. Sometimes it's because I don't have the emotional energy for the threat of physical harm or even just the awkward stares. At other times it's because I just don't want to. My ability to be fluid with my gender, to be inconsistent, is my right.

I'm aware that I have the privilege of being a gender chameleon, choosing how I express my gender and how I am perceived. Many folks don't have that choice. In some ways, I choose more feminine expressions because that makes me less threatening than being seen as a Brown bearded terrorist. While at other times, I lean into my masculinity as a shield against homophobia and transphobia. And when I am assaulted while traveling for a little too much sashaying, left with a bloody face and feeling violated, it's a stark reminder that neither presentation is enough and both are too much for the world around me. I am a threat to the culture around me simply because I choose to express myself in ways that make me happy. This is the complexity of living at the intersections, I am always having to make calculated guesses on how to present myself in ways where I can be authentic and safe while navigating the broader systemic restrictions on how I am perceived.

Even writing this piece has taken me over a year. I've been wanting to write it but the fear of naming my feelings in this way seems threatening to my relationships and cultural notions of gender that have been hard-wired into my being. I have spent days just staring at an empty document... wanting the courage to be me, to speak about my journey and to name these experiences. Given the tumultuous world we are in and the hundreds of other unjust socio-political happenings, I felt guilty about naming my need to be addressed by my pronouns. Then I realized that I cannot be a full human being and advocate for so many other issues if I'm not able to even share my own voice.

I use they/them because it liberates me from the boxes of masculinity and femininity, challenges my internalized toxicity of masculinity and pushes me to be comfortable in the unknown space of being both/and, of being in what Gloria Anzaldúa calls *las fronteras/the borderlands*. I've also just learned the pronoun "kin" as an option and I'm exploring it. Kin comes from English and German roots, meaning family or tribe. Somedays, I like "he" but find myself struggling to deconstruct if that's because I actually like that pronoun or if it just makes it easier for others, reducing my own anxiety of being constantly misgendered. Thankfully identity is a journey and not a set destination so I can continue to explore.

We have the power to undo and rearrange our sense of self with every breath.

As with many forms of privilege, pronouns may seem trivial for those that hold culturally normative gender identities and expressions. For those of us in the borderlands, pronouns have the power to solidify or shatter our sense of self.

14 THE TERRITORY OF THE HEART IS PRICKLY

The territory of the heart is prickly.
Like a wild cactus,
forgotten,
dusty and

                                         entangled upon itself.

What is the purpose of this existence?
Messy, dehydrated
and reaching towards

the Sun.

"The wound is where the light enters." Rumi

What if the entire heart is wounded? Can the light hold my
wound? My pain? My healing?

While my heart feels   lonely,
I am not alone.

I am in a desert full of other beautifully prickly beings,
learning, healing, growing, belonging.

The snake of my soul
sheds this thick skin,

unlearning
these
        traumas, messages and voices that have gotten stuck on
my soul over time.

It is the prickliness of my heart that allows my much-needed
shedding to manifest.

Without the prickliness, like the cacti surrounding me, where
would I be? Is healing even possible?

The territory of the heart is prickly with purpose. Each thorn.

Protecting,
catalyzing
        and weathering many sandstorms.

The prickliness is sweet and juicy with potential. The prickliness is resilience. And even full of light.

This wound is not a source of shame but a symbol of my strength.

Each prickly piece, a reminder of my journey towards peace.

15 READER'S ART: WHAT IS YOUR HEART TELLING YOU?

Making art has always been a useful way for me to slow down my overthinking and elevate feelings in my body. My art is often not planned out but intuitive. I sit, meditate, drink some tea and start putting pen to paper.

Take a few moments to reflect on whatever feelings are swirling around in your body. Don't think and just start drawing on the next page. See what emerges. Cover as much or little of the page as you'd like. There is no correct approach to this process. Feel free to take notes afterwards of what feelings, stories, or "Aha!" moments came up for you.

RAJA GOPAL BHATTAR

16 DEAR APPA, HOW IS IT POSSIBLE TO MISS SOMEONE I DON'T EVEN REMEMBER?

My aunt, sitting in a dusty rose colored sari, is cutting some fresh green beans as I sit on the tattering gray rug by the TV, asking why I can't just go back to India to be with my mom. It had been a few hard weeks at school with bullying and not fully understanding the American education system. So far, the U.S. was not all what I was told it was going to be.

"Just ungrateful. You know you weren't even supposed to be born!" she states as if it's a dirty little secret.

"Huh?" I'm confused.

"You know your Appa was happy with just three children and you... you were unexpected. Your Amma was still very young but was clear she wanted to go ahead with the pregnancy. Your Appa on the other hand was in a bad place. He still hadn't gotten over his first wife's death but had been convinced by the family to marry your mom for the sake of having someone to raise his two children. And then your sister was born and everything was good. A few years later your Amma was about three months pregnant with you when they got into such a sharp shouting match. It felt like watching an intense Bollywood movie.

'We have three already, why do we need another?' your Appa gripes.

'*Yenri*? What do you mean?' Pleads your mother, 'You know I love them, but I also want to keep this child.'

'But we are already struggling and do we really need another mouth to feed?'

My aunt brings me back to the present, "You know your Periya (her husband and my Appa's older brother) and I had struggled for many years to have children and had always wanted a male child so we had someone to do our death rites. And that's when we told your Appa, 'If she wants to keep the child, let her. You don't have to be so stubborn, Ranga. Maybe it's God's will. And if needed, we will take care of the child. You need not worry!"

"And so your Appa was still upset but we supported your Amma through the rest of the pregnancy. He didn't talk to her for that whole time. They huffed around each other with as little interaction as needed and it felt like his mind was lost in some deep hole."

"You were born on a Sunday morning, early actually, which is funny because I can't get you out of bed anytime before 8am! But not that day. You arrived in the wee hours of the day and reluctantly your Appa came to see you and your mom."

As is tradition, children are not given names until twenty-one days after birth but only referred to as Baby. Once the Jatakam, an astrological birth chart, has been created based on the planetary alignments at the time of birth, family elders would gather to discuss naming options which would honor family ancestors and begin with auspicious sounds for the child's wellbeing. My Appa didn't want any part in this process, she says. Somehow they waited on naming me well after the twenty-one day period and I was still just Baby.

"Your Appa was just busy caring for your other siblings, especially caring for Nidhi and his disability. I think your father always felt guilty that they missed giving your brother his Polio shots in the chaos of caring for his ailing wife. And when Nidhi started needing intensive care and resources, your Appa struggled to balance everything. Your Amma never lost hope and kept praying that he would come around but she found herself in postpartum depression as well so it was a sad sight. Except for your Akka, Manju. She was the happiest big sister I've ever seen! She would not leave your side and kept asking when you would get a name."

"She woke up from a nap one day and wouldn't stop pestering your Amma about a name. Manju decided that you had plumpy cheeks and big eyes so you looked like a prince. She started calling you Raja (a favorite term of endearment for Indian babies). And it stuck. You became Raja. Unofficially of course since your Appa died soon after followed by a year of mourning. Your Amma couldn't make sense of life. Was she to find joy in her kids growing up or sad at becoming a widow at just twenty-one years old?"

Widowhood is a curse in a culture that not only isolates widows but also demonizes them as bad luck, denying them any joy. I don't wish anyone this curse having witnessed the way my Amma has been treated by family throughout my life.

"Raja was just too generic and your Amma wanted a name with divine meaning, so she started calling you Rajagopal - the king of the cowherders. And it stuck." The king of the cowherders? Another name for Krishna, a god who grew up playing the flute while the cows grazed the fields and known for his playful and mischievous tales but always protecting the villagers and animals.

Coming to the U.S. meant people butchering my name over and over which eventually lead me to make Gopal my middle name and just Raja as my first.

I don't often talk about my upbringing because it's painful and I'm afraid of inadvertently shaming my family, yet this is *my* story. To be clear, I am grateful that I live my life today because of this journey and there are parts that are still unspoken, unexplored and unhealed because it is just too scary. While I never knew my father, people often say I have his features and his temperament.

Here's one of many letters I would have sent him:

Dear Appa -

How is it possible to miss someone I don't even remember? I sadly have no memories of you, unlike my siblings and everyone else in the family. There is so much mystery and history around your death and all the events that have manifested since. I can't believe you died over forty years ago. And who would have guessed I'd be alive, writing this letter at the same age as you when you died? Finally voicing all the things I've ever wanted to say and the many questions I have for you.

So many questions.
No responses.

What were you like: What was your favorite color? What was your vision for the world? What was the happiest moment of your life? Nidhi says you were a tall man with a presence as you entered any room. Pale skin, dark brown eyes, thick black hair, huge black rimmed glasses and your uniform of white kurtas and the day's newspaper under your arm. Even as a child of five, Nidhi remembers your helplessness on your death pyre, a stark difference from the man you were in life. Manju just remembers you bouncing her upon your thighs and making silly sounds. I wonder what Kirti remembers of you. We don't have a relationship where I can ask her that.

What were your demons? Why did you choose not to name me? What would you have named me if you could have chosen? Am I not worthy of having my name? Of having my name spoken in all its depth, love and aspiration? Will I ever be enough for a father that died before seeing me grow up? Or enough for a mother that can only see you in my face?

Amma... Amma remembers you as a sad and angry man who experienced a lot of pain in your short life. While love was never a word that was used by her, I can't imagine what you felt for her. I just have been told by her and others that you didn't want me. While I may have been an unwanted accident, I know I was not a mistake. Yet what made you so angry that you didn't talk to Amma for most of the pregnancy? What was the purpose of causing so much emotional pain to a woman who had given up everything for you and lost herself with your death?

Some say you died of a heart attack. Or was it a broken heart? I can't imagine how one recovers when the love of your life dies and yet has to keep living. Is that why you didn't want me? Or is it so that I didn't have to face the harsh realities of a world not built for me. For so many years, I have resented you because you didn't want me. Feeling like from inception I have navigated a world where I am always on the edge, never in the middle. Feeling unworthy. Feeling lost. Some say you chose to end your life, wanting to be with your true love. Is this what love can do? I'm not sure exactly what happened but still there are whispers of a woman's death followed by a man's heart break followed by a woman's suffering followed by a young child lost across seven seas.

And in a sad and strange way, your death became a life source.

Without your end, there would have been no beginning for me. I would not have been adopted and brought to the U.S., had access to the education and opportunity to pursue my own joy. I never will know who you were, yet I know who I am in this life, in this context and I'm grateful for your role in getting me here. I have surrendered my anger towards you. I wonder what parts of me are from you? What parts from Amma? What a disturbing existence to have one parent dead, the other alive, yet both strangers. Are my flaws from you? My resilience from you? My idealistic world vision from you? My sadness from you? Will I ever be gentle with myself enough to accept that you are a part of me and still guide me from whatever world exists beyond death? Will I ever know exactly what happened to you? Does it even matter now? What do we lose when we move to different worlds? What do we gain when we go beyond familiar waters? What wounds are deep enough to be carried across oceans and lifetimes? What is my healing? What is our healing?

Do you hear me all the times I talk to you? It's nice to think that maybe you are out there in the Universe, guiding and supporting me. Doing in death what you could not do for me in life. I've been told you were a visionary and started a progressive newspaper as India was being birthed, were involved in politics and were stubborn about what you wanted. By pursuing that which makes your heart happy. I'm like you in that way, you know? It's a part of me that I love. I am so proud of the ways I have navigated life so far. Is this the vision you had for me as you reported on the struggle for freedom and civil rights? Belli Moda, Silver Cloud - the name of the newspaper. It held a sense of hope, finding a sparkle in every cloud. Can a cloud, gray and pregnant with stories, be the source of freedom and joy? Can the rain wash away the pain? Can the days ease away the questions?

I will continue talking to you, asking questions and living my truth. I hope I get to know you better by knowing myself. May we both be gentle with ourselves on this journey. May my healing liberate you and all the ancestors.

Sincerely,
Rajagopal

17 TURNING PAPER INTO PRAYER

At the temple, an older grandpa brings colorful stationery,
Teaching little Indian kids how to make magic out of paper.
"Origami, an ancient Japanese art of transformation," he says.

A fold here, a fold there and voíla! A lotus! A box! A crane!
While that gentle grandpa's name is lost to memory,
I can still create a crane with ease.

On a ship, Bo and I meet. He oversees service projects while I
support the spiritual growth of the students. He, a white man
in his 60's and me, a queer Brown person in my 20's.
An unlikely friendship while sailing the Atlantic Ocean.

Our ship, headed to Japan, was diverted due to the tsunami
and we are all heartbroken.
Some for not being able to visit Japan as planned

and others for the death and destruction experienced by innocent people of the land.

"Let's make 1,000 Peace Cranes," says a student, making
sense of the grave event.
A community healing project,
a token that can be sent to the people of Japan.
Since the Atomic Bomb attacks during WWII,
a young Japanese girl's wish transformed
paper into prayer.
Paper cranes blossoming into symbols of peace.

I remember teaching Bo and others:
Fold here, and there, then tuck the flap,
Massaging pieces of paper into a creature that can fly.
His big hands struggle but persistence wins over.
By the fifth crane, he's got it down!

We make cranes everywhere!

At breakfast,   and   at meetings,
    during classes,   over lunch,   or watching a movie,
            before card games, after dinner,
                even while having
                tea on the deck,
                and in bed.

We bless the birds.
1,000 cranes ready to fly,
carrying interfaith prayers of peace.

Years later, Bo and I meet again.
Reminiscing on the avian adventure
that fostered our friendship.

He now leads communities in service projects around the
world.
Their symbol, the humble paper crane.

"From the time we made all those cranes," he says, "I realized
even a piece of paper
can become
a messenger of peace.

And that's what life is about,
transforming everything into peace."

Even a piece of paper can become a messenger of peace.
How many papers in the world are simply crumpled and
thrown away?

What a gift to learn that with some love and folding,
paper can learn to fly.

Constellating joy out of chaos.
If only more people could be like paper.

Paper, from a tree
becomes a bird,
flying home,
preaching Peace.

Thank you, little girl, for your wisdom.
Thank you, gentle grandpa, for this gift.
Thank you, dear friend, for this reminder.
Thank you, peaceful bird, for turning paper into prayer
and people into peace.

PAPER CRANE

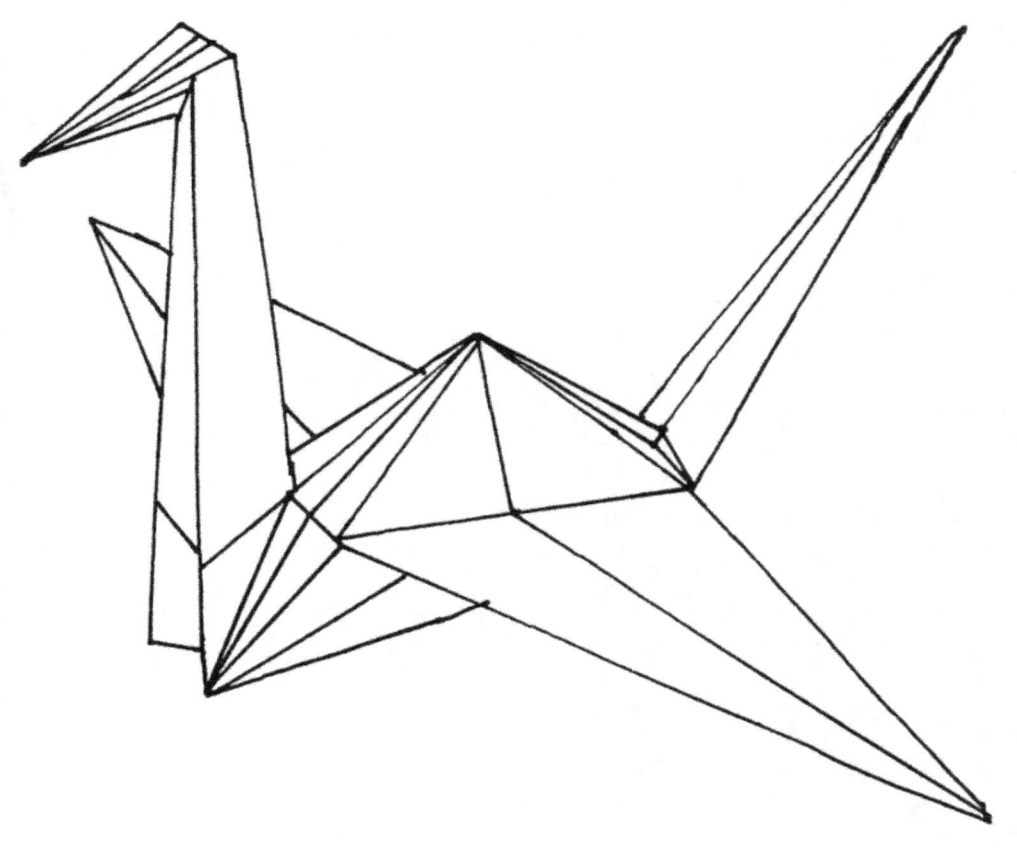

18   K-MART KID OR HOW I GOT AN "AMERICAN" ACCENT

Being a third grader was not fun. I was bullied regularly by peers and older kids, the scary fifth graders. Everyday it was something: my misfitting clothing (mostly from Kiran, the son of the other priest at the temple and practically my best friend... well, only friend, but that still makes him best right?), the fragrant Indian food for lunch in old margarine containers or my strong "Indian" accent, having moved to the U.S. just two years earlier. None of me fits in with an elementary school in Calabasas, California, home of rockstars and rich white people... and a Hindu temple on a hill. We were living in a trailer home that was at the back of the property. It had faded yellow walls and horrible tube lights that made even the color yellow look depressed. And, if you were lucky, sometimes the lights would flicker for days, like a dilapidated disco not ready to give up yet. It had one bedroom on one end, a "dining room" which was a 70's diner style round table and four chairs covered in brown vinyl. On the other end was a bathroom and a kitchen with two hot plates and a small fridge, bigger than a mini-fridge but not a grown up fridge either. All the appliances were a beige-brown that made sure everyone knew they were original features of the home. I didn't really understand it then, but living in a trailer home in one of the richest cities in the country gets complicated... real quick.

Awkward, shy and friendless, starting third grade in a new school, new city, new everything... .all pretty awesome so far (insert as much sarcasm as you can muster). Everyday was an adventure in being reminded of my un-Americanness. Kiran was also at the school but he was a year older so I didn't get to see him much, not even at recess since we had different recess periods. I loved Mummy's cooking but it was getting harder and harder to eat food at school. I had classmates make faces of *ew*'s and *what is that?*'s on a regular basis. At least in Illinois, I could eat lunch by myself in the classroom, but here, they only had lunch outside. Who does that? Guess that's what you get for having a family that moves to California.

We line up to go to lunch and proceed outside where I take a seat on the small cement bridge to nowhere at one end of the playground and start to enjoy my meal. Billy, a white boy with messy brownish hair, was the first to start picking on me. I am enjoying my Mummy's famous bisibelebath, a delicious stew of rice, lentils and veggies mixed with the most fragrant spices in the world, when I hear, "What is that? Poop! HAHA!" First, I'm a bit confused then I realize he's talking about me and my lunch. I don't know what to do so I just stay quiet. And his laughter gets louder, I don't see any teachers around and I'm no match for this kid and his buddies that all look like a scraggly 90's boyband in the making. I scarf down my lunch and spend the rest of recess right by the classroom door and keep tracing the cursive embroidery of my name in golden thread on a cherry red jacket I had just gotten. Around the playground I see kids laughing over a game of four-square or playing tag as they run over and under the little cement bridge. It makes me feel safe to be by the door even if I'm annoyed that I can't be on the bridge which has the best view of the playground. Why did we have to move? I was just getting comfortable with school in the Chicago suburbs and now my days have come to this: avoiding a bully named Billy on the playground.

Ms. T, my teacher, was nice enough but never figured out how to say my name. *Raw-sha* was the closest it ever got. What else can you expect from a white woman who grew up in the Valley? She says, "Class, time to come back!" and I scurry in and take my seat while all the other kids bemoan having to end recess so we could actually learn something. Next day, we line up for lunch and recess. I go stand towards the front given my "B" last name. I hear two girls snickering behind me, Kathy and Jo. The former is taller than most of the boys and lanky in her pink polka dot dress and matching bow in her hair while the latter has on light blue tights and a gray sweatshirt with the "POLO" logo across the front accessorized with a dozen colorful candy bracelets up her right hand. I don't pay attention as the teacher is getting people into line but I hear the girls say, "Yeah, Kimmy told me he shops at K-Mart and is really poor," says Kathy, "That's why he has to bring a smelly lunch in a recycled box." Jo responds with "I mean, yeah. So sad!" and they continue giggling. I keep my head down and proceed to lunch, my usual spot by the door where I hoped the teacher could hear me if I screamed loud enough.

Being called K-Mart Kid for my hand-me-down and generic brand clothing caused lots of ridicule and shame that I couldn't understand. The only stores I knew were K-Mart and Bradlees and I preferred K-Mart because it was usually cheaper and I didn't feel as guilty for asking to buy a pack of gum or a t-shirt when we were there. Mostly my clothes were still what I had gotten from my cousin Krishna when we left Lemont and from Kiran's mom or some random temple member who wanted to get rid of their kid's clothes. I never really cared about clothes much since I never had any choice in what to wear. Since we lived in a trailer, there wasn't the best air circulation and everything smelled like Indian food - a mix of turmeric, chili powder, cumin, curry leaves, and a little hint of brown sugar that covered every surface. So my clothes smelled like Indian food too and it was comforting to me whenever I missed my Amma or my siblings, I would just smell my clothes and feel like I could hear them.

The daily social isolation of lunchtime and pain got so bad that I began throwing away my food or "forgetting" it on the bus. It was so easy to fool immigrant parents and Mummy couldn't understand why suddenly I was eating so much food when I came home from school but not gaining weight. Once I figured out the school offered free *American* food, I pleaded and forced my parents to apply for a free-meal program through the school cafeteria. They were hesitant but finally gave in after a week of pleading. While many kids of a similar working class background may have been ashamed about getting free lunch, I. Was. Ecstatic. It was one of my first attempts at being "American enough". What could be more "American" than white bread PB&J sandwiches, CocoGrahams and chocolate milk?! Now, I think of how scared and tired of bullying I must have been to try so hard to prove that I was enough. American enough. "White" enough. Human enough. I'm sad for that child enduring unnecessary self-measurement and self-hate within suburban white bread neighborhoods of America for years to come. How much of this child's life was about being enough to exist?

And then there was my accent. I remember Billy once coming to me during recess, folded hands and a Starbursts candy wrapper placed on his forehead like a bindi repeating, "Thank you, come again!" in a ridiculous accent and shaking his head side to side, like Apu from *the Simpsons*. I had never watched the show since we only had a small TV with a built in video cassette player and grainy local channels in the trailer, so I had no idea what the heck he was doing. I would shake my head, mimicking him and pretending everything was fine. One day, he came right up to my face as if he was going to jump me. I freaked and went to the teacher crying. I had been taught to be ashamed of crying by my family, but I knew I felt better whenever I had cried and I just didn't want the scary image of Billy with folded hands and shaking head to take over my nightmares. Ms. T. called Billy in from recess and made him apologize to me. "I'm sorry, *K-Mart*", he said that last word just under his breath. I was so angry but couldn't do anything with the teacher standing right there. I let it go because Mummy had said, "Be like Gandhi, Let Karma take care of him." I sighed. *What did Karma know about being an awkward Brown queer immigrant?*

One day Ms. T told us that we had won the school's reading contest and were getting free pizza for lunch the next day! I couldn't believe it. Soon after coming to the U.S., a family friend had taken us to PizzaHut for dinner and since then I was in love! I mean what's not to love about greasy cheese, sweet tomato sauce and veggies? That was the only time I had ever eaten pizza, since my mother believed that if you didn't eat three Indian meals a day, you weren't Indian (and it was a way to save money). So this was going to be a sacred treat. In class Ms. T asks everyone what slice they will have, "I'll go through the roster, and just let me know what you will eat, cheese or pepperoni."

"Jessica?" "Cheese, please!"

"Byron?" "Pepperoni!"

"Cassie?" "Pepperoni"

"Jo?" "CHEESE!"

"Billy?" "Obviously the best, pepperoni!"

"Raw-sha?" "Um.....Pepperoni, please!"

"Kimmy?"...

And so on. At the end of the day, Kiran and I get picked up by my Daddy as usual and jump in the back seat. "How was school?" Daddy asks.

"Great! You know we are getting pizza for the class tomorrow and I ordered pepperoni! I'm hoping it will be a spicy pepper or something. I love a good ve... "

"Um... you know what pepperoni is?" interrupts Kiran.

"Yea, a vegetable, duh. It's *pepper*-oni.

"No, silly. It's meat! So stupid."

"Don't call me stupid, you stupid."

"Okay you two, stop it!" yells my Daddy and we stop.

I couldn't sleep that night as I had images of all the kids eating their pizza and me sitting with my one slice of meat pizza. The next day I'm off to class and it's raining. As soon as I see Ms. T, I run through the drizzling drops to plead with her to change my order as I'm a vegetarian and can't eat meat. "Let's see what we can do," she says and we get on with the morning lessons. As lunch time approaches, I am nervous. The pizza arrives and Ms. T announces to the whole class, "OK everyone, so we have cheese here and the pepperoni line there. Now remember, you each get one slice only. Oh and would anyone who ordered cheese be willing to switch with Rah-sha since he can't have pepperoni?" Seriously? Does she need to give these little monsters any more reasons to make fun of me? I was mortified. This was not a good day. Thankfully Jess agreed to switch and I got my cheese pizza slice. It was oily with that fake cheese powder on top and smelled like America. I took the piece and headed outside to my usual spot on the bridge to enjoy this delicacy. I pick up the piece awkwardly since it's too big of a slice for my eight year-old hands and can already taste my deliciousness as I take a bite... WHAM!@#$&*$(#. It's both slo-mo and super fast, all at once. It's like watching a cannon ball fall out of a window.

My face feels steamy and cold, oily and wet. I realize I'm in a puddle under the bridge and the pizza is making out with my forehead. It takes me a few minutes to get up, soiled with dirty puddle water and pieces of cheese hanging from my hair as I look up. Everyone is staring at me and at the end of the bridge, I see Billy and his bully gang trying to hold in laughter. I start crying and hear him say, "Hope you enjoyed the pizza, sucker!" I lose it. I can feel the blood rushing up to my face and I'm glad for a moment that my brown skin doesn't betray me and no one can see how red I feel. I am just weeping my heart out and start running towards the laughing boys, I turn into my truest bullish Taurus self, butting Billy in the stomach with my big head as if horns had grown with a determination to maul him. Billy is a bit out of breath before he starts pulling my hair as I'm now flailing my arms to cause as much harm as possible. We hear Mrs. T. yelling, "Stop it, you two! Right now!" I look up, cheesy hair, snot and tears dripping down my face with dirt and leaves stuck all down my soaked clothes. We both get sent to the Principal's Office. She asks me to recount what happened and as I start the story, she says, "Wait, can you slow down. I'm having a hard time understanding your accent."

I just started crying, not being able to see that she was just trying to get the story, and full of rage for being in this place, far away from everything I've ever known and utterly miserable. I wonder what Amma is doing right now? Is this punishment for something I've done? I learned at that moment that I have to change to survive in this new world. I commit to losing my "Indian accent". Is an accent determined by the purity of pronunciation in line with British colonial residue or the ability to sound like a fictional cartoon character portrayed by non-Desi actors? Or does anyone who is ethnically Indian automatically have an Indian accent?

I spent years peeling away my accent - words and sounds from a colonizer's language, one self-hating moment at a time. While I was proud of my "American" accent as a teenager, and as a college student in a 9/11 world where my accent was proof I wasn't one of *those* terrorists, I've realized over the years that my linguistic assimilation was an intentional process to be "enough". Enough to survive Billy and his bully gang in third grade. Enough to survive mean teenagers in high school and all the people that have said, "Oh you don't even sound Indian!" What does that even mean? I know my "American" accent has often given me cultural capital; defining me as more civilized or not "too Indian" while also questioning my authenticity of birth in India due to the lack of a recognizable "Indianness" in my speech.

Billy and I both got detention for a week and I had to write a letter to the Principal about how I would never use violence again. It was the most half-assed letter I've ever written. For a child who was always told to let things go or to just suck it up, this was a moment of self-preservation and resistance. Now, everytime I eat pizza, I feel that little child inside jump with glee and victory.

Growing up in a home that told me I'm ugly, my nose is too big, my skin too dark and my queerness too much, and a world that told me my accent is too much or not enough, I have spent my life trying to fit in and to be just enough... .just queer enough to not be too much, just brown enough to not be American and just American enough to not sound "Indian". Still now, I get annoyed when I'm told I'm not Indian because of my accent and yet being reminded I'm not American because of my skin.

Always too much and never enough. Now my heart aches for the eight-year old kid, just trying to survive in a new world filled with trailer homes, hand-me-down clothes and pizza on my face.

19 ALWAYS TOO MUCH AND NEVER ENOUGH

Dear Ma,

At some point around fifth grade, I started calling you Ma, short for mummy but also a bit more Indian. For me it was a sign of getting closer to you since I had lived with you and Daddy longer than I had lived with my Amma in India. But I remember the day I realized I would never be enough for you.

I had just come back from college for the November break and your niece Lavanya was visiting with her one-year old child. I had recently told you that I was no longer interested in being a Pre-Med major or in pursuing a career in medicine, law or engineering. You said that I obviously couldn't be a lawyer since I wasn't assertive enough to even make it through one semester of college without falling apart. It didn't matter to you that I, as a Brown queer person with facial hair, was just still surviving. Clutching my humanity as the world labels me as a terrorist in a post-9/11 world and required me to grow up even faster than I already had. Seems to be the theme of my life, Ma. Maybe I just have to keep growing up quicker than my age to stay alive.

I remember sitting on the old hand-me-down couch in our living room. An apartment inside the Woodbury Apartments complex on Summer Hill Road. I was on the couch doing some reading for my Psychology class while you and Lavanya were chopping vegetables. Her son was just bouncing in a baby rocker in the corner.

You were still mad at me for having changed my major and were always so good at projecting your anger. "Don't be a failure like Raja. What can one do with a psychology degree? You should be a doctor or something useful," you say to the clueless toddler. It stings. Does changing one's major and envisioning my own future make me a failure? Or is it just failing to uphold your expectation of me. I couldn't tell if you were more angry at the change in major or at me for making a decision about my life without your consultation. Was it a betrayal of your American Dream? Was it that my life not being bound by your words was too much for you?

You said it so simply, "You'll always be a failure. What a waste to bring you here and spend all this time and money on you. We should have just left you in India to fend for yourself. You've become too American, like all these spoiled kids here." So I was just an investment? It was not the first (or last) time you would say such things but something broke in me that day and I find myself still putting those pieces back together.

Thankfully, my own journey has let me shed these moments of your voice ringing in my head, telling me to stop being myself. I love you, Ma, but I love myself more. Our greatest achievement is being true to our hearts and I pray that in this lifetime or the next, you have the peace to love yourself and those around you for who they are and not for who you need them to be.

I love you and I know, in your own warped way, you love me too.

- Raja

20   LIFE IS LIKE THAT

I overheard a friend say, "It's ok, caterpillar. You will be a beautiful butterfly one day if you are patient"

But no butterfly is possible without the caterpillar.

Admire the caterpillar, not because it will someday become a butterfly, but for its innate wisdom and wiring to protect and transform itself.

Forming a chrysalis, capable of chiseling new life into itself.

The beauty and suffering of the caterpillar
Is what gives beauty to the butterfly.

Wisdom before,
wisdom after.

Suffering in between.

Beauty before,
beauty after.

Resilience in between.

If we ignore the beauty of the caterpillar
we sacrifice our ability to see the butterfly's beauty.

Life is like that.

21 KRISHNA ON A CHRISTMAS TREE

Growing up in the U.S., all around me, Christmas was a big deal. Though it was only one day in December, it was talked about, advertised and decorated from about September through January. All my friends, neighbors, and every retail establishment seemed to think Christmas was an opportunity to puke lights and glitter all over the place. I can't actually remember my first Christmas in the U.S. but I think it was uneventful because my father always had to work at the temple. As orthodox Hindus, it was just another day at the Bhattar household.

It wasn't until we moved to Connecticut and into the temple that Christmas became "a thing". Yes, I am the kid who wanted to celebrate Christmas, the most Christian of holidays, on the grounds of a Hindu temple. Doesn't it feel like the most "American dream" experience? We lived on the temple premises upstairs above the temple in a modest apartment with three bedrooms, the smallest kitchen in the world and a large high ceiling living/dining/common space.

I don't actually remember how many years we lived up there, but it was a formative part of my growing up. As the only priest of a small yet established temple, my Daddy and Ma were fully involved and ever present in the temple. Living right upstairs meant that we were available for people to just come knocking even outside of posted temple hours. My favorite part about living in this apartment, beyond having my own room, was the large circular window that overlooked the parking lot and neighborhood. There was an old 1970s couch that had been given to us by some temple devotees just below the window. I loved sitting on this couch. I would read, do homework, study my times tables or my Kannada grammar all while looking out onto the world beyond the temple. This is where we could see who is coming and going into the parking lot and also observe the beautiful leaves changing color in the Fall and snow falling in the Winter, late at night lit only by the streetlight in the dead of winter. It was this window that made me fall in love with Winter. Being able to watch the silence, peace and beauty, while enjoying the warmth and comfort of being inside, wrapped up in a blanket.

Just around the corner were my favorite neighbors, The Murphys. Shelly and Dan Murphy were proud first generation Irish Americans, who had grandchildren my age. I would sneak through the bushes separating the temple and their backyard to hang out regularly with their grandkids, but always enjoyed the conversations with the grandparents more. I wasn't really into sports, girls, trucks or other interests that white straight boys in suburban Connecticut were into. Go figure.

It was at the Murphy's house where I learned to love Christmas. For almost a decade I got to partake in the rituals of getting ready for Christmas. I got to help Shelly put out the full ceramic village, consisting of a post office, ice rink, town square with a colorful Christmas tree, cotton snow, little white figurines and all the accouterments that come with a "white christmas". We would put pine garland on the mantle, electric candles in the windows, wreaths on the doors, and my favorite part was always putting up the Christmas tree in the family room. Coming from a tradition deeply rooted in rituals and cultural practices, Christmas is one of the few times that Christianity made sense to me. The act of decorating your house with all these little dolls and houses felt like celebrating Navaratri in our family where we put up gollu (a display of religious statues) and decorating the house felt like how we celebrate Deepavali with lights and candles all throughout the house. The overwhelming amount of food covering the table, felt like any family celebration in India with a wide array of colorful dishes, ready to be devoured. But the Christmas tree was unique. It was one of the first times I got to watch a white family, almost as if in a sociological experiment, get ready for this important holiday. I remember one year they bought a Christmas tree almost 10 feet tall and equally wide. Helping to put up the Christmas tree was quite fascinating as we tried to secure the base of the tree into the tree stand and avoided getting stung by the sharp pine needles. But my favorite part was decorating the tree. I would watch as the family would go through boxes and boxes of ornaments, everything from hand me downs to ornaments the grandkids had created to pieces that they had picked up on their travels around the world. Watching and being part of this annual ritual was comforting but made me sad for all the rituals, life events, and annual family traditions that I miss out on by being on the other side of the world which felt like living in a different universe.

When I was in eighth grade, I remember sludging through the snow, towards the temple, after spending the day hanging out with hot cocoa and decorating the tree. The beautiful circular window just looked empty and sad and I decided something had to be done!

"Daddy, Why can't we get a Christmas tree like the Murphys?"

"Well, we're not Christian and in case you didn't know, we're living on top of a Hindu temple."

"I know that... but aren't we the religion of pluralism?"

Thankfully, a year earlier, some of the temple leaders had noticed a need for a Hindu festival to counter/complement Christmas, Hanukkah, Solstice and other festivals this time of year. The annual Kalpavriksha Day was a fun celebration that was the pure form of diasporic creativity. The Kalpvriksha is a tree that emerged during the Hindu story of creation, where Hindu gods and demons churned the milky ocean representing the Universe using a mountain as the pole and Vasuki, the snake as a rope. It was the ultimate fight of good versus evil. In the story, the Kalpavriksha tree emerges just as butter emerges through a process of churning cream. I loved the creativity of taking a plastic Christmas tree and Hindu-ising it with all of our colors and symbols. It was complete with a turtle tree skirt that represents Vishnu coming down as a turtle in the story to keep the mountain from sinking into the bottom of the ocean along with the various different images and resources that were churned up, creating the world that we live in. As each part of the story was read by a narrator, young children dressed up in various costumes would come up, take an ornament and place it on the tree. Collectively creating this intercultural manifestation of immigrants, navigating our own mythologies and roots, while intertwining them with rituals of our chosen land.

So as I stared at the empty window, I decided we needed our own Kalpavriksha Tree in the circular window for everyone to see. My parents were quite hesitant, but given my persuasiveness, we went to K-Mart and bought a 4-foot plastic Christmas tree with all my savings and some help from my parents and of course, lots of twinkling lights. The couch was moved so the tree could sit right in the middle of the circular window on top of an old computer box so that it would fit perfectly, and could be seen all the way from the front entrance of the parking lot. The white lights surrounded the tree and lined the window, creating an opening into this diasporic immigrant experiment. My parents were adamant that it could not be a "Christmas Tree" and therefore we had all ten forms of Vishnu towards the top of the tree, along with angels, covered with little Indian jewelry, other gods and goddesses, and all of my mom's jewelry and my dance jewelry I could find. While the temple's community hall displayed the Kalpavriksha tree with all its stories, this tree was not a Kalpavriksha tree. It was a Hindu Christmas Tree. Big distinction. This was one of my earliest lessons on interfaith creativity, finding ways to honor various traditions while still upholding our own values and philosophies. We even had baby Jesus in a manger and a menorah strategically placed at the bottom layer of the tree to make sure everyone knew where they stood in the social strata of our home. While we wanted to honor them, my parents made sure it was clear that Hinduism was the dominant tradition in this house. My favorite element of the tree was the angel. Yes, she was pale and had blonde hair, but her white dress was overlapped with silky, colorful material, small sparkly jewelry, and a tasteful yet prominent bottu on her forehead as she watched over the various mythologies sprinkled across the tree.

Traditionally, every evening, my mother would light two little silver lamps at the family altar and take a small silver plate with the lamps to offer aarti prayers to all the different images of gods, goddesses and saints around the house as a way to honor them and bring good luck. With the new tradition of a tree in our window, we created hybrid rituals too. As we lit up the tree every evening, Ma would ask me to do the aarti for the tree and the various Hindu gods and goddesses, and even the baby Jesus in the manger. I remember a non-Hindu friend visiting our house, and wondering what all the different images were. "Oh yeah, it's just Krishna on the Christmas tree with all his friends." The look of confusion on her face was priceless!

And while we didn't celebrate Christmas, we always found a way to get a few gifts under the tree. Usually Christmas Eve meant I would spend hours alone in the temple, decorating and dressing up all the deities for Christmas. Well, it wasn't technically for Christmas, but because many people had the day off, the temple would be busier than usual, and so we took time to celebrate with a special set of decorations and outfits.

Before I went off to the temple, my parents and I would have a special meal of puliogare and gulab jamuns (my favorite dishes) for dinner. We would even leave some gulab jamuns for Santa by the tree, even though we didn't have a fireplace and the gifts were already visible under the tree. The sweets became my late night treat once I came back from the temple in the wee hours of the morning. On Christmas Day, we would open gifts in the morning and see what "Santa" brought this year. Usually it was warm clothes I needed for school or some money in an envelope that said "From Mr. Santa Claus". With gifts unwrapped, and the tree glowing through the window the day would begin with our prayers at the family altar, and then a long day working at the temple for all of us: Daddy performing pujas, Mummi cooking all day and me rotating between helping both of them. Being in the diaspora, bridging roots from the homeland and branching into our new world, an attempt to be fully ourselves in the both/and.

22 (RE)DEFINING LOVE: A JOURNEY

Love seems such a gentle word. Affection and care. But what
is it in practice?

I first learned that love is about sacrifice.
Watching Amma in her sorrow of widowhood yet smiling and
waking up every morning for the sake of her children.

Next I learned love is about compromise.
My sister shared the seventeen rupees after breaking open
her clay piggy bank so that we could both get a Cadbury's
Chocolate bar.

Then I learned love is about loss.
Watching the family cry over Roji Akka's death was so sad,
even for a five-year old just learning about the realities of this
world.

Fourth, I learned that love is about joy.
On a plane with my aunt to an unknown world. The stress of
what's ahead was easily overshadowed by the unbelievable
sight of clouds and stars just outside my window!

Next I learned love is about learning.
Learning new ways to be with my aunt and uncle. Learning
their patterns, going to new schools, speaking new languages
and doing everything perfectly to make them proud and
happy.

Then, I learned that love is about friendship.
Making friends as an awkward, skinny, Brown kid was hard
but those I met in elementary school became friends who
have supported me through so many eras of life.

Further I learned love is forbidden and shameful.
Accepting myself and my desires while being told I was
broken by the world. At home and at school, always friendly
yet never fully myself for fear of losing all that I knew in the
world.

Next I learned that love is a history.
Learning about queer and transcestors and their myriad
stories, knowing I have a deep lineage of queerness blending
into and emerging from my brownness.

Then, I learned that love is liberation.
People have fought for me to be here and my presence.

Loving is what will make way for future generations to feel safe and accepted.

Ninth, I learned love is action.
Protesting on the streets, counseling students, advocating for better policies. Creating the world that we can imagine together.

Finally, I am learning that love is about letting go.
Letting go of the need to be seen by others as I see myself.
Letting go of people who cannot celebrate my love. Letting go of my own notions of what "real" love is.

Love is not at all. It is complex, messy and beautiful, all at once.

My love is what feels good to me and who I am with.
My love is queer. My love is healing. My love is sacred.

23 BOYS DON'T DANCE

There I am in the temple basement staring through the narrow window in the double doors, just wide enough to peek into the auditorium, where rows of Indian girls and teenage women are dancing to the beats of a wooden stick hitting a wooden block. *"Tha Ki Ta, Tha Dhi Mi, Tha Ki Ta, Tha Dhi Mi..."* Padmini Aunty and Radha Aunty drive up from New Jersey every Sunday to spend hours teaching groups of these girls and women dressed in a rainbow of salwars, sarees and tights. In the back of the room, I notice my friends Lakshmi and Priti dancing along with each beat. They look a bit clumsy, but I guess that's natural for a first dance class. A whole hour passes. I can see the cacophony of hand gestures as the body shifts down to aramandi (a diamond shape of the legs with heels together with knees pushing away) to various jumps, kicks and kneeling postures. The cassette tapes keep getting rewound as they practice the same sequence over and over. I keep looking over my shoulder to see if anyone is watching, as I try to mimic the hand gestures and hum along to the tune.

"Where were you after the puja today?" Asks Mummy.

"I was downstairs watching the dance class. It looks so cool! I saw that Lakshmi and Priti have just started too! *Nannu Bharatanatyam kaleebhodha Ma?*"

"*Neenu dance kalitheeya?*"

"Yes, I want to learn how to dance!"

"*Dance hudugarigalla!*" Dance is not for boys.

That stung deeply.

"*Yake kaleebaradhu?*" Why can't I learn? I pleaded.

"Well boys just don't learn dance, especially not Bharatanatyam. That's for girls and in any case, we can't afford it. You should be focusing on your grades."

"Mummy, I'm an honors student and I'm only in fourth grade!"

"Still grades matter at every grade! And you got a B on your maths test last week. You want to get into Harvard don't you?"

"I don't think Harvard looks at fourth grade test scores, Ma. And if my friends are doing it, why can't I?"

"I don't have time for this. Go do your homework."

"Mummy... ."

"Nope. Just go."

A few weeks later

I can't stop spending my Sundays with my face pressed so hard against the little window, it feels like I might fall through it. For my birthday, I had asked for a walkman and after some nudging and a coupon I got in the newspaper, I had a neon blue Sony Walkman! I felt so cool! I would grab a few of Daddy's carnatic music CD's and listen to them late at night in bed, choreographing moves based on what I had seen through the window that week and imagine I was performing for Padmini Aunty, who was a famous movie star, dancer and the primary teacher.

At school that week, Mrs. G mentioned that we would have a world culture fair to celebrate all of our respective traditions and food and everyone had to find a way to participate in the event. I somehow agreed to dance. I spent several sleepless nights choreographing and figuring out what to wear. I decided to wear my prayer robes of white cotton with a thin blue border, a white t-shirt, one of Daddy's shawls around my waist and my black velcro sneakers. I really didn't know what I was doing but I knew the song by heart and dancing made me feel seen for the first time by many of my peers. As luck would have it, the local newspaper covered the story and posted a picture of me in the paper in a Ranganatha pose, kneeling on one knee while stretching out the other with my right hand curved above my head and my left hand stretched as if I was lounging.

At school that day I was so excited to see my picture in the paper but got really nervous about showing it to my parents. They had been clear that boys can't dance and would probably chastise me for wasting study time on this foolishness. Why couldn't Mummy and Daddy see that this is important to me? Even our bus driver Leroy had commented on the article and expressed his pride at learning more about my culture.

That's the day I learned that Indian parents (at least all the ones I knew) loved it when others praised their children, and if it was in the paper, even better! My parents must have bought two dozen copies of the paper and even sent laminated copies to India for all my family to see. To my surprise, my parents showed the paper to Padmini Aunty that Sunday and her face lit up with joy!

"You look just like Nataraja - the god of dance," She exclaimed, "I've noticed you peering through the window each week. Are you serious about learning to dance?"

"Yes! But... .Mummy said boys don't dance and that we can't afford it."

"Well, if Nataraja, the god of dance, is himself a man, why can't a boy be a dancer?!"

Whoa! How had I never thought of that? I couldn't hold in my grin!

"And if you are serious, I'll talk to your parents and we'll work it out."

That was it! She agreed to teach me for free as long as I committed to practicing and showing up every week and didn't let my grades slip. I was in heaven! I was the only boy in the class for all eight years and got to perform in beautiful silk outfits, sparkly jewelry and even learned how to play with makeup! It was the beginning of my queer awakening. Throughout the years, I would spend sleepless nights choreographing dances of queer love stories.

Bharatanatyam is a several thousand year old dance form, mostly from south India, that blends Hindu mythology, Carnatic classical music, and colorful outfits to recount various mythologies. Traditionally it is performed inside Hindu temples and village celebrations by Devadasis, women who married God and spent their lives as artists. In the diaspora it has become a middle class Desi path to cultural education over the last 70 years.

It is believed that Shiva, one of the primary Hindu godheads, was dancing his Ananda Tandavam - a dance of joy - in the form of Nataraja (literally, the king of dance). After years of penance, Sage Bharatha is given a boon to witness this dance and transcribes the various elements into the Natya Shastra, a text that serves as the foundation of Hindu dance forms. Traditionally, this dance was carried through teacher-student lineages of Devadasis, female dancers who were "married" to God and preserved the art.

24   LOVING MYSELF IS THE HARDEST THING

I
am
here.

Right here.

And have always been here.

Sparkly, complex, factual.
My dear heart, the mirrors on the wall are not to be trusted,
for they only show the self which others have taught me to see
in myself. How can such a fleshy image be so inaccurate?

Yes, the image in the mirror is deceptively accurate in the
wrinkles, gray hair and brown skin. But the mirror cannot
fathom the moments of laughter that have given birth to wrinkles, medals from a life of joy.

It cannot capture the luck, and even divine gift, of a life.
A life long enough lived to see gray hairs on every surface
of skin. Each gray line on my brown skin is like a tree that
has matured enough in the brown earth to bear fruit.
juicy, full of flavor and a sign of life. What a gift it is to
breathe enough life into this body to see gray, like much-
needed clouds heavy with rain on an unbearably
sticky day.

Kintsugi - A Japanese art that rebirths shattered pottery by
filling cracks with gold and silver. An act of love that refuses
the disposability of this vessel, this body, this heart.

Nothing is ever broken so deeply that it cannot be healed
with love and care.

A fresh piece of pottery may reflect a new life, a new vision
yet a pottery that is
reunited - pieces and precious metals,
reclaimed - body and soul,
rebirthed - pleasure and purpose found
cannot be captured in a simple reflection.

Loving myself is the hardest thing to do.

Stop depending on the reflection in the mirror and love what
is - even when I cannot see all of me.
Ditching the envious mirror
made of others' shoulds and coulds
for this life I am living.

I
am
here.

Right here.

And have always been here.

No mirror is able to capture the lines of gold and silver, like
rivers of healing - an intuitive reminder that my love for me
is not in spite of the cracks
but
because of them.
Like silver lines against brown skin.

Rumi proclaims, "The wound is where the light enters." So a
vessel without any cracks is no vessel at all but simply a show
piece displayed on the mantle.

That is no life - to be seen yet not enjoyed. Such is the fate of
a mirror. I can see but I cannot be.

To see but not to be.
A book may be valuable unopened on a shelf, but what life is
that for the book?
No, let my life
be the book that is read, reread, and covered with notes in
pencil on the edges;
little dog ear creases, holding a million secrets from moments
in time,

of laughter, of tears, of living.

Let my life be
the broken pieces and the glue,
the the pain and the joy, and
the secrets and the truths.

Oh don't be fooled, my heart,
gold and silver do not give value to the vessel,
the vessel gives value to these metals.

Healing my past has brought forth my inner precious metals
to shine. Gold and silver sparkle brighter against the richness
of my ancestral brown skin. Nothing is added, nothing is
removed.
Simply reclaimed.

Each crevice, a signpost on the journey to myself. Krishna
emboldens Arjuna, "It is better to be yourself in all your
imperfections than to be someone else perfectly."
Our true duty is to see and fully embrace our lives.
All the signs of aging and mortality,
against all the creams and crazes.

Gray hair, like streaks of comets across a moonless sky.
Wrinkles, as we see every detail of the Full Moon on a clear
night.
And my Sunkissed brown skin - embracing hues of the Earth.
These elements have more stories to tell
than can ever be witnessed in a mirror.

Dear envious mirror, why are you green? Loving myself used to be the hardest thing to do and now I love each scar, each metallic manifestation of truth, each sign of living.

I
am
here.

Right here. Beyond any mirror.

And have always been here.
Nothing added, nothing removed.
Simply reclaimed.

I am.

25 NEW YEAR'S EVE

New Year's Eve. 11:30pm. While other kids my age are at home getting ready to watch the ball drop in Times Square, I'm in the temple, inside the central shrine, the garba gruham. Even though I'm in high school now, this is how I spend most holidays decorating the moorthies for various festival celebrations throughout the year. Meaning literally "embodiment", a moorthy is a representation of a deity, made usually of stone, wood, or metal, which serves as a means through which a god or goddess may be worshiped. Having grown up in a family of pujaris and moving around the U.S. so my father could be a priest, I spend most days in the temple too. Even as young child, I regularly helped out with handing out flowers or helping recite various Hindu mythologies as part of religious rituals and helping with alankarams, dressing up the various statues with colorful fabrics and jewelry. Having been my dad's helper for so long, I've now become the "official decorator" for the Gods, usually working late at night by myself. It's my favorite time to be in here; most of the lights are turned off and the heavy smell of the lamp's oil, camphor and agarbathis linger softly around me. Once they figured out that I could lose myself for hours at the temple, my parents justified it as a great outlet for me to be "creative and still Indian, thankfully without all the nonsense of school plays and extracurricular groups or partying like *those* American kids. Chi, chi, chi." (These last sounds were often relayed with vigorous head shaking in disapproval.)

I could be creative and expressive in my alankarams because it's what traditional Hindu priests are supposed to do and therefore didn't freak my parents out or make me "too feminine." But I've also recently started taking Bharathanatyam classes which they're not as comfortable with. I guess dancing around on a stage with lots of make-up and jewelry in colorful silks just isn't their definition of what Indian men are supposed do. What they really want is for me to play tennis with all the other Indian boys that come to the temple or go to my school as if throwing a stupid ball around the court with these cocky, testosterone-filled guys is gonna help me become more "normal" in the community. They want to be more like *those* boys, you know, the ones that score 1600s on the SATs and get into all the Ivy Leagues while winning tennis matches and living the American Dream. The boys that come from doctors and engineers and probably will become doctors and engineers only to breed more doctors and engineers. That's just sooo not me! How can I become that when I come from twenty generations of pujaris. I don't even care about Ivy Leagues, let alone *know* what the heck they are. I've just been told by every Indian aunty and uncle at the temple that that's where I'm supposed to go if I want to make it big in America and make my parents proud.

At home, every free moment is filled with statements of, "You better study good or else... " or a regular recitation of my mother's running list of things they left behind in India so I could have this opportunity to study in the "greatest country in the world."

When I'm in the temple, there is a peaceful silence and calmness, broken only by the Carnatic music cassettes I have playing in my little pink boom box. Satyanarayana, the temple's main moorthy and namesake is still unclothed. Well, I've tried on three different outfits on him and didn't like any of them so I've taken them all off. A rainbow of saris and dhotis and glittery jewelry are scattered all over the floor as I'm scrambling to figure out what to do. I'm getting frustrated as I can hear the slow ticks of the wall clock but I'm happy. Decorating so many moorthies alone is no easy task, but I prefer to be by myself in this process. This is my time. Our time.

This is when I talk to all the moorthies. To me, they are like children or younger siblings who can't dress themselves yet. I put on what I think will work, but I can quickly sense if they're not happy, so I pull everything off and start all over again until I feel like they look *just right*.

While I like playing dress up with all the gods and goddesses, my favorite is Satyanarayana. Lately, the time it takes me to decorate this moorthy seems to take longer and longer every time. I find myself mesmerized by this statue, whose name translates to the God of Truth, as I just sit there staring. The black stone beautifully contrasts with the vivacious colors of his garments and jewelry. Just witnessing how the light reflects every embellished detail of this statue's body is captivating. He may be cold as stone to the touch yet he is also the embodiment of the warmth and beauty of life radiating through his smile and sparkly eyes. Sometimes, I wonder why we hide such beauty with all these garments.

I've never shared this with anyone, but I am only able to stare because I know my Satyanarayana won't mind. Looking at him makes me feel a sense of calm that I've never felt anywhere else. In these moments, it feels like He was created just for me, just for this one moment of our connection. My walls of manliness crumble, giving into emotion as our energies become one. This is when I know I am alive, as are my feelings.

I've been having a lot of feelings lately and not sure what's happening to me. It's not the butterfly-like feeling... it's more like an earthquake, a force I can't control that seems to take over and destroy me. When this happens, my feelings are hard to decipher and I feel so ashamed, thankful my brown skin hides my fears from the world. I've been wanting to stare at many of the men that come to the temple and I find myself trying so hard to not be obvious about the feelings in my stomach. It feels nice to admire them but then I feel like I'm doing something unholy.

Even at school I often catch myself staring at the boys in my class even though they're all just awkward and pimpled teenagers like me. There's just something about them that makes me want to stare but also behaviors that I can't seem to understand. How come none of them are ever looking at me? And at the temple, I become speechless around boys that I've known for years but still find it strange to see their gangly yet muscular teenage bodies as we run around the parking lot but then they all start talking about girls and I wonder why I don't have those feelings. All the aunties also keep asking me if I have a girlfriend yet. That's just funny because my parents have told me to never even think about having a girlfriend. They say, "It's just not something *good* Indians, like us, do." Don't worry, I don't think that will be a problem. Here's the thing...

I think I like guys.

Sigh. There, I said it. *Whew.* That wasn't so bad. Right?

Right.

Why is this happening to me?! I do all my prayers and come to help at the temple every day. I'm supposed to be the good Indian boy who marries the good Indian girl waiting for me in the motherland, and make good Indian babies. Lots and lots of babies. I like kids a lot but does this mean that I can't have children ever if something is wrong with me? How can I? I've never heard of a Hindu gay person before let alone someone like me having kids. No, I'm not gay. This is just a "thing" that guys go through. That's what my brother says, and he's 7 years older than me so he must know these things, right?

Even with all these strange feelings, when I'm with my Satyanarayana, I don't have any fear. When I am alone with him in the garba gruham, I can talk to him without hiding anything. I can tell him he is beautiful. I can kiss him, his stony lips against my warm lips. I can call him mine. I'm sure this would not be cool if my parents found out but didn't Radha, a young maiden of Hindu mythology, become so engrossed with Krishna that she would dress up like him so she could become one with him? And didn't Krishna come to her each night in her dreams because of his love for her? Didn't Andal do the same when she would make garlands for Ranganatha and try them on to make sure they looked good? Though everyone told her it was offensive to Hindu traditions to love god that way, in the end Ranganatha transforms from stone to human, just to marry her and make her immortal. My love is just as powerful yet I see no examples of my kind of love. May be this is not a love that god allows? But then why do I have these feelings? Where are they coming from? Can I just stay here forever with him so I don't ever have to face the world again? I don't think about these fears when I'm here, just staring at my Satyanarayana.

Midnight. A new year has begun. If only, I could become immortal this year.

26 READER'S PAGE: AND AT THAT MOMENT I RECLAIMED MY LIFE FOR MYSELF

Dear Reader -

Whether we like it or not, life is always happening. And if we are present, we can find moments to reclaim our life, centering what is important and letting go off all that is not serving our wellbeing.

The Buddist Teacher, Thich Nhat Hanh, says that we all have a five-year old version of ourselves inside our body that is ready to heal. If we approach ourselves and those around us as we would a five-year old version of themselves, we could lead with such compassion and care. This is your chance to write a letter to yourself at whatever age you choose. What would have been helpful to hear at that age to heal? To feel safe?

Get comfortable, make yourself a nice cup of tea and talk to your younger self.

Take three deep breaths and feel your memories connecting with your body.

Breathing In, Breathing Out - Relax your body
Breathing In, Breathing Out - Listen with your heart
Breathing In, Breathing Out - Open your eyes

Remember this does not have to be perfect or coherent to anyone else but you. Just write.

Here's a suggested last line for your story:
... and at that moment, I reclaimed my life for myself.

Dear Younger Me at the Age of:
By:

27 MIX CAKE MIX, WATER, OIL AND EGGS

I'm a cook, I am not a baker.

I learned how to cook from Mummy, since she used to cater for the temple and people in the community all the time. We lived in a two bedroom apartment in a housing project. She had a little propane stove that we would place outside on the little patch of grass, just behind the apartment. And being an orthodox Hindu family, we were strict vegetarians, and still are. In our home, there was no meat of any kind, no mushrooms (fungi is considered to be unclean and flesh-like) and no eggs (since an egg could have become life if fertilized).

As a middle schooler, I had become involved at this amazing community theater in our town that drew kids from all over the state! I loved dancing and acting as a kid, and I was getting into the theater scene, where I was finally making some friends. One day, I got super excited when I saw a poster for a four-month West African dance and drumming course that was being offered! I was able to convince my parents to let me sign up for yet another afterschool commitment, received a scholarship, and paid for the balance with whatever money I had saved up from helping at the temple and my part-time job at a local grocery store.

The teacher was a Black woman dressed in a flowy, colorful, print cotton outfit and her locks gathered up in a beautiful head wrap. She was friendly and patient as we started to learn some basic West African KuKu dance steps and danced along to the Djembe drum beats. The sexy shirtless drummer, who was probably in his early 20s with beautiful dreads and the nicest arms I've ever seen in my life, definitely made the painful dancing and complex choreography more enjoyable.

Week after week, I loved learning the different steps and symbolisms, and got excited when we learned that there would be a culminating performance to show off our skills. After one of our rehearsals, the teacher said, "So I'd like us to have a small reception after the last performance next week to celebrate all your amazing work! And it would be great if everyone could contribute something to this potluck. If anyone likes to bake, it would be wonderful to have a cake or any other goodies!"

I had baked a little bit in my life. Usually eggless cookies or a simple banana bread but that's about it. I looked around and no one was coming forward to bake a cake and in my sophomoric wisdom, I said why not, "I'll bake it!" I was excited to learn something new. As a first time cake baker, I figured going from scratch was not a smart idea so that weekend, I borrowed Daddy's car and drove to the Stop & Shop to pick up two boxes of Betty Crocker's Super Moist Double Chocolate Cake mix. Using a trusted and true American classic should be easy enough, right?

I looked at the instructions on the box and realized there was a problem. It said "just add water, oil, and eggs!"

Water? Check. Oil? Check.

Eggs.

Oh crap. How am I going to bake this... with eggs... in my purely egg-less house? I quickly devised a fool-proof plan, or so I thought. I would buy the eggs on a separate transaction so there would be no evidence, ask my neighbor if I could store it in their refrigerator and on Saturday bake the cake while my parents were busy at the temple so it would be ready for the reception!

Slight problem, I had never bought eggs before. I stood at the refrigerated shelves of eggs in the store and must have looked like I was staring at an alien because this random white grandma slows down her shopping cart behind me and asks, "Are you okay, hun?"

"Umm, yea. Just trying to figure out how to buy eggs. It's my first time." I felt like I was deciding on which condoms to get to lose my virginity. Thank the Gods my brown skin hid my embarrassment.

"You mean you've never bought eggs before?!"

"Yeah, it's a long story." I really didn't feel like explaining the intricacies of Hindu dietary restrictions and philosophies to a rando at the grocery store.

"Oh you just check the eggs and you're fine."

"Check the eggs?" How might one do that? I thought to myself.

"You just open the carton like this," she gestured, "and make sure none of them are cracked."

"Oh, of course. Cool. Thanks!" I picked up a 6 pack of eggs and got out of there as soon as possible along with two foil pans and dark chocolate chips and chocolate frosting. There can never be too much chocolate.

My neighbor was totally fine with storing the eggs. On Saturday morning, I convinced my mom I could not go to the temple because I had to study for an exam. She didn't ask any questions and I offered no responses. As soon as she left, I ran over to Irene's apartment to get the contraband and got ready to bake a cake!

Actual instructions from Betty Crocker:

> 1. Heat oven to 350°F for shiny metal or glass pan or 325°F for nonstick pan. Grease bottom only of 13"x9" non stick pan or bottom and sides of all other pans.

Easy. Done. I used the oil spray to coat the foil pans.

> 2. Mix Cake Mix, water, oil and eggs in a large bowl

with mixer on medium speed or beat vigorously by
hand for 2 minutes. Pour into pan.

Ok seems easy enough... wait a minute. Do I just throw the eggs in whole? Do I need to prepare them somehow? Is it just the outside parts or the insides too? Do they need to be cold or at room temperature?

Hmph.

I finally accepted that I had no freaking idea of what I was doing, but it was too late to turn back now. I couldn't let down everyone in the show who would be looking forward to having cake that evening. Unlike today, I couldn't just Google something on my smartphone to figure out how to navigate this dilemma. I decided to use my intuition and placed three full eggs into each of the batters, breaking them in half as I had seen done in countless Food Network shows. I added chocolate chips for some extra texture, mixed everything together with an electric blender and got them into the foil trays.

3. Bake as directed in chart or until toothpick inserted
in center comes out clean. Cool 10 minutes before
removing from pan. Cool completely before frosting.

Finally, the easiest step. I baked the cakes as directed, and after about thirty five minutes the toothpick came out clean. The house was filled with the smell of warm gooey chocolate, and it was heavenly! Once the cakes were cooled, I took time to cut the cake into the shape of Africa and covered it with rich dark chocolate frosting and decorated the top with a little flower in Western Africa to honor the origin of the dances we were about to perform.

I was so proud of myself for making this delicious looking and smelling treat. I covered the cake with saran wrap to keep it safe, using some toothpicks to prevent the frosting getting stuck on the wrap. I cleaned up the kitchen, gathered all the evidence of eggs into a plastic bag and discarded them in the dumpster at the end of the block to ensure it was untraceable to an awkward, orthodox Hindu, Brown kid in apartment 108, and got to the theater to dance.

The last performance was electrifying and just so much fun! After the curtain call, we all headed downstairs for the reception. People started cutting slices of the cake along with all the other food that was being served and we were generally having a good time. I had a piece of cake and it truly was luxurious - super chocolatey, crunchy and moist!

A little later in the evening, the sexy drummer came up to me. "Wow this cake is sooo delicious, Raja!"

"Oh, thanks! It's my first time baking!"

"No way! Seriously so good. Especially the M&Ms in there! I love the crunch!"

"Well I did put chocolate chips in there and maybe you're tasting the eggshells... " Now I'm nervous and start to sweat...

"That's a good one! Haha. You're funny, dude. Who would put eggshells into a cake? Haha"

"Yeah, you know me. Funny as a bunny!" Funny as a bunny?!?! Who says that? What the hell is wrong with me?!

Oh my Gods. I was mortified.

What have I done? Will people die from this?!? Why didn't the instructions say no eggshells? How am I supposed to know that "three eggs" means everything but the shells?!? Even the picture on the box shows three full eggs. Thankfully the metal blender had pulverized the shells into tiny pieces. At this moment I was so grateful for my melanated skin which prevented people from seeing all the blood rushing to my face out of embarrassment.

I called my friend and fellow dancer, Maria, over, "Hey... so random and totally hypothetical question, can people die from eating a whole egg?"

"Whadyu mean?"

"Like the shell and stuff."

"Oh, I don't think you're supposed to eat it but I don't think it'll kill ya. Why are you askin?"

Whew. What a relief! "Oh, no reason. Just curious. Thanks. You, my friend, were awwwesome tonight!"

I couldn't sleep all night. The next day, I hung out at the library and searched the internet for answers and asked my friend's mom, the Home Economics teacher: "Hey Mrs. K, Can I ask you a question?"

"Of course. What's up, kiddo?"

"So, I baked a cake this weekend for the first time and the recipe called for three eggs... so I put three eggs into the batter and baked it."

"So what's the problem?"

"Well you see I put the insides, eggshells, and everything in. Will that hurt someone?"

She was trying so hard not to burst out laughing. "Oh I see. Well, a little bit won't kill ya, especially since it was baked so no risk of Salmonella but probably safe to just not do that in the future."

"Thanks Mrs. K."

And so that evening after school, I got home and decided to fess up to my crime and called the theater to talk to Ship, the artistic director.

"Hey Ship, can I talk to you about something?"

"Sure Raja. What's up?"

"So you know the cake I baked for yesterday? Well... ." and recounted the whole story and he just started laughing.

Don't worry. The very next day, I enrolled for Home Economics for the following quarter and haven't baked with eggshells since!

28 I HAVE ALWAYS BEEN THE HOME I SEEK

I am proudly gender queer.
Whether you find me GNC enough or not
My pronouns are they/them and and my gender is trans-
forming
Gender is bigger than cultural norms or clothes that can be
bought
It's a sense of who I am that is more complicated than a
binary of how men and women should "be"
There are as many genders as there are leaves in a forest of
trees
It's simply a concept, made by cis-het men
To oppress anyone breaking the binary, i.e. trans, gnc or
gender fluid like the breeze
The truth is: gender is universally open
To interpretation and embrace
My gender is a beautiful, colorful and complicated truth to be
freely spoken

A liberation that gives us all grace

To be who fully ourselves, expressing our style
I am me and I wear what makes me happy
In a sari, in a suit with a train that goes for a mile
Or in a scarf or some heels or something a bit more chic
Like a strapless black velvet dress
I look quite cute, making my own knees weak
Lipstick on point and makeup is flawless
I have always been the home I seek
Looking hot off the press
I am now naked and happy
Bearded, eyeliner and a booty to boot
Centering my happiness does not make me sappy
I am at home in a dress, a t-shirt or the chocolatey darkness of
my birthday suit

Growing up I was told my queerness was too much and nose
was too big
My skin too dark and my features too ugly for words
I've learned I've always been beautiful, the color of a tree-
ripened fig
With features beyond words,inspiring beautiful love ballads
Sung by the birds
My queerness is my weapon and my armor
May you also be brave enough to explore the breadth of your
gender
Taking you from this sad but safe binary harbor
As you embrace a life more tender.

29 I'M NO LONGER CERTAIN GOD EXISTS HERE

Such a strange feeling. I'm in front of the temple for the first time since my Daddy was fired three weeks ago. Well, he was asked to "resign", but same difference. I can feel my heart beating and my blood pulsing... especially to my clenched fist. The door is closed but I can see people mingling inside through the glass panels. There's Vikram Mama (*mama* meaning uncle and a term that's used indiscriminately to any older man) behind the counter helping someone... why didn't he help my Daddy? After all that my family has done. We've spent the past fifteen years at this damn temple. Dad has never gotten a raise though he, and Mom and I, have put in thousands of hours into making this place the community it is today. When my Pa got here there were only three pictures and one room and that's it. Now, there's an actual temple with so many moorthies, altars and space. I should feel angry but I don't. I'm just sad.

I grasp the handle as firmly as I can... its cold metal sends chills down my already shaken body. As soon as I pull, the silence of the outdoors vanishes into a sea of different languages, parents yelling at children, men chanting, women making garlands and the priests getting ready for the weekly bathing of the statues. My body goes forward but my heart jumps back and wants to hide away somewhere. If I could just become invisible, I would never have to see these people ever again. In my brain, I keep seeing all the auspicious days he has spent offering special pujas and all the late nights we spent getting ready for one celebration or another and the years of our lives we have given to this place. My father is a weak man, I know, but he is a genuine man. It's something I have always appreciated about him. Though Ma tells him to "Do this" or "Don't do that," he often goes to his own beat. Pouring his heart into this place and people that come through. Seeing all these people around just makes that realization even more painful. They have used all his energy and now, once the temple is up and running... they want us to leave. How do we leave fifteen years of sweat and love just like that? I'm probably too young to be thinking this but I feel like I should be advocating for my parents and somehow get him his job back. Isn't that what I need to do as a good child? Though I was adopted they've always treated me like their kid and yet I feel helpless to support them in any way right now.

A woman in a green sari sees me by the entrance as she's exiting but quickly looks away. Does she know? I wish I could just be invisible right now... but I want to see my Satyanarayana (the main deity of the temple) along with all the gods. I've decorated all these moorthies since we moved here and even if I'm not allowed to do that anymore, I want to see them. I want to speak to them, as I used to when I was in high school. Suddenly, I am a stranger in a temple where I know every floor tile and crack in the ceiling. Why is this so hard? It feels like it's my first day of school again and I'm that kid that has just moved here from some other planet. I can feel sweat gathering at my temples while my hands try to let go of the door handle and rush to grab my dhoti, trying to get back into my body. I am looking around and though everything looks the same, nothing feels the same as it used to. I used to love coming to the temple, a place where everyone knows me as Raja, the Priest's kid, and now I am entering as Raja, just another temple visitor. My heart wants to run directly into the Graba Gruham, the main sanctum, so I can close the doors and cry my heart out, but even that feels strange now.

I don't want to talk to anyone so I just walk past Vikram Mama and ignore him as he's calling my name. I go directly to ring the bell at the entrance to the Ganesha sanctum. I remember this bell being put in; I was the one that decided it should go here rather than in the front lobby area. This is my favorite bell of the three in the temple. It was donated by one of my former dance teachers so ringing it always reminds me of her but more importantly I love its pitch. It's the perfect sound that just makes any thought in my head go away. I would usually just jump into the sanctum and offer my personal prayers and flowers while fixing a piece of jewelry on the statue but now it feels like trespassing. Even Ganesha looks sad today as I take the aarathi and start my pradakshinas around the shrine. The cold tile feels so weird under my feet. Because this temple was an addition to the original plans years ago, it never got the heating pipes like the rest of the temple so it startles me every time. From out here I can't see the inside of the dome above the shrine. From inside, I could see my name etched into the concrete from when I helped the artisans from India as they were building the shrine. It's somewhat comforting to know that it will be there long after we are forgotten in this place but I wonder if anyone else will notice it at all. I wish I could go back to the construction of the temple so I could etch my parents' names into the temple as well so that someday someone would know who lived and breathed the temple into existence. I start thinking about the first Ganesha Chaturthi we celebrated after the temple was inaugurated. I stayed up until 4am the night before getting all the decorations ready for the morning's puja. Ganesha just looked so beautiful. I remember sitting there for almost an hour just staring after the puja was done because I wanted my brain to capture every detail of the moorthy.

I feel my eyes starting to get wet and don't really want anyone to see so I quickly run into the storage room but even that feels strange. The strange smells of coconuts, puja spices and cleaning products overlapping are really strong. I always hated that smell, but today it's oddly comforting. I've never been in here without a purpose before. Usually, I need to break coconuts or wipe up a spill or grab extra plates for the puja. Now, I'm just standing there being overfilled with anger and helplessness; I can feel steady streams of tears covering my face. This is just silly, I'm twenty-three years old. I shouldn't be crying. This was never *my* temple. It was just a place where my Daddy worked (even as I had that thought, I knew it was a lie. This place has been our life for many years and I feel a sense of ownership).

I hear the puja starting so I try to pull myself together and head out of the closet. I step into the main hall and I feel everyone staring at me, even the moorthies. I can't imagine holding my tears in long enough to offer my usual morning prayers at each shrine so I go straight to the main shrine. I see Madan Mama, the other priest, starting to take the first pot of water by everyone so that it can be touched and blessed before being poured on the moorthy. I used to do that. It's very eerie to just be an observer after years of being on the other side. It's almost like having an out-of-body experience. Ever since all the drama happened last week, I haven't spoken to Madan Mama. In fact, it was him who told me about what happened at the Board of Trustees meeting. How did he know so much about what happened at the meeting when he wasn't in the room? Almost instinctively, I look away as he walks by with the pot of water. I feel rude but whatever. I am angry at Satyanarayana. Why would you do this to my Dad? To us?! After all we have done to foster this community in your honor. I have so many things I want to yell at that piece of rock! I just can't believe that a "real" god would allow for something like this to happen! I mean my Dad has worked his butt off, all his life and what does he have to show for it? Nothing. It used to be the respect we had within the community, but now even that is gone.

Mommy can't stop crying around the house and yelling at my Daddy for not working harder, but I know she's saying it out of her own pain. Pa just sits there through all her rants and doesn't add much to the conversation. Every now and then, he'll try to say something in his defense about what happened at the meeting but none of that is of comfort to her. He was taken by shock with the, "It's not you, it's just that we are going in a different direction with our priestly needs." What does that even mean? Daddy has stopped being himself since last week. He sits in front of the altar in our home and performs all the pujas but his soul is missing. Mommy hasn't gone to the temple since this happened either. I know it's really hard for her after fifteen years of going at least three times a day but she sees this as punishing God. She's always been such a strong person and comforting source in our family that seeing her in such a mess is frightening. I don't even yell back like I usually do when she says something about picking up my clothes or finishing my prayers, which seems to get her even more upset. So even saying nothing gets me in trouble! Go figure.

I hear my name. It's Madan Mama, now with a pot of milk for blessing. I touch the pot; the warmth of my fingers curves around the silver pot of cold milk. Part of me wants to just pull at it and spill the liquid. I don't know if there is a God anymore but if there is, then this piece of stone in front of me is surely not it. I'd rather have the milk spilt on the floor than carrying the false hope of all these devotees to be poured on that statue. I let go and he moves to my left so that others can touch the pot. My mouth goes dry and I start feeling guilty for thinking such horrible thoughts. I don't know if my guilt is for wanting to waste milk or for questioning God. Either way, I don't really care. I can't sit here and watch this charade. I want to be in the Garba Gruham, the main sanctum, yelling at the statue. Or go to the sanctum next door to talk to Goddess Lakshmi to talk some sense into Him. But obviously I couldn't do that with all these people here so I just get up and leave. I don't even look back, like I usually do. My Mom taught me that I should always glance back before leaving a temple because we shouldn't go away from God, but I'm no longer certain God exists here.

30 I JUST WANT TO WEAR MY SKIN

I just want to wear my
skin.

Brown
Ashy
Hairy

I am all the things I was taught to not find beautiful.

Yet,
Here I am.

Beautiful
Authentic
Happy

I have become all the qualities I have come to admire in my community

Maya, a friend's daughter once tried to scrub her skin in the bath so she could discard the melanin and become a "pretty white girl". Though any amount of scraping cannot remove the ancestral history and wisdom gifted to us by Surya, the Sun, who transforms skin into a

Brown fortress of resilience and joy.

Moisturize. Adding oils and other lubricants to the skin to keep it shiny and even. The ancestors within our cells yearn for water, moisture and nutrients that glimmer like gold in the morning Sun.

Nourishing
my skin
is
a prayer,
a rejoicing of my ancestral right
     to exist in this skin,
          in this body,
               in this time.

Like my skin, my hair has always had a complicated relationship with me. On one hand, I began losing hair on my head in high school making me question my masculinity and attractiveness. And shaving it off on a random Tuesday in June fifteen years ago was a liberation I didn't know I needed to live and see

The beauty of my bald head.
Immediately slightly discolored from years of being hidden by follicles of hair yet now bronzed to perfectly match the rest of my skin. Magic.

In Hindu culture (and Buddhist and others), shaving one's head is a renouncement of earthly attachments to beauty standards. And confusing for my family who struggle with why I choose to live this life in this "way". Everytime I am asked, I find it a reminder of my choice to live my life in my truth, embracing my ancestral roots, living a vision that the Spirits have dreamed into existence. Every time I hold the razor, I am reminded of how shaving my head has become a spiritual ritual,
where I offer
prayers
as I commune with God in all their glory.

Offering my shaven spikes of hair in gratitude for this life. And a chance to balance out the hair on the rest of my hairy body. Being a gender queer person is so divine and strange. I am labeled too masculine if I shave my head but too feminine if I shave my arms or legs. A simple ritual becomes an act of rebellion. I am too much and too little and never ever enough.

I just want to wear
my skin.

Beautiful
Authentic
Happy

Being enoughly enough.

Prayers in flesh.

Of sometimes ashy and sometimes moisturized layers. I want to be naked, touching and tasting the stories hidden in each wrinkle, each shaven follicle and each chocolatey skin layer, just as I am. I want to feel Surya on my skin and feel the browning of my ancestral wisdom, just like a bird sibling innately knowing how to fly or a turtle kin knowing how to crawl towards the sea.

PRAYERS IN FLESH

31 THE DAY I REALIZED I'M BROWN

It was supposed to be an ordinary Tuesday.

Where were you on 9/11? If you were alive in the U.S. in September 2001, you probably remember all the details of the day, as well. I was in my regular Tuesday morning lecture in the Charles Hayden Memorial Building of the College of Arts and Sciences. My friends and I are half asleep or doodling as usual, pretending to listen to some old white professor talking about some obscure topic, when the Core Curriculum director interrupts the lecture.

"Dear students, There is some troubling news happening right now. The World Trade Center in New York has been attacked by terrorists. All we know is that one of the planes left from Boston... "

Terrorists, planes, attacks. Terrorists, planes, attacks.

"... Please stay calm. The News is still trying to figure out what's happening. I urge you to contact your families and check in on them. Classes are canceled for the day. Please be safe. We will send out more info as it becomes available. Good day."

"Good day"? Who says that on a day like today?

Classes canceled, eyes absorbing graphic images 24/7 from all the TVs in the student union. I could feel Death and Fear lingering amongst us. I could not fully grasp what was happening at all. The scenes on TV kept showing planes running into the buildings, the towers collapsing and people jumping and fire and debris everywhere. It felt like a horror movie rather than live news.

After about eleven hours of watching the news and tragedy unfold, I walked back to my residence hall and kept over-hearing people. "...terrorists... ", "...Muslims... ", "...bastards... ", "...savages... " "...war on terror..."

My head was spinning. I couldn't sleep and most of the other residents of the floor ended up in the common room, talking. Some people talked about friends going to school in New York and not knowing if they were ok. Others spoke about family friends still missing and still others worried about the Chemistry exam scheduled for the next morning.

The next few days are a bit blurry to be honest.

Between vigils, news-binging sessions and homework for my first semester of college, I was numb... even when I got stupid questions from idiots in my classes or in the dining hall:

"Wait, aren't you Muslim or something?"

"Did you know those guys that blew up the towers?"

"Are you a terrorist?"

"What does your name actually mean?"

"You're not like *those people, are you?*

"Are you a suicide bomber?"

So many questions from strangers for a nineteen-year-old with no answers.

They said it so casually. What I wanted to say was a snarky "Yes, I know them. Actually they're my uncles" but instead I said nothing. Then when a friend asked me similar questions during a study session and I bit back, "Ummm no. Are you crazy? I'm not Muslim like *them,* I'm Hindu. We don't do that stuff." At that moment, I didn't realize how terrible my statement was.

Growing up in a conservative Hindu community and in a predominantly white part of Connecticut, I never knew I was "Brown." I mean I knew I was not white or Black or Latine but I had grown up only thinking of myself as Indian, Hindu (and often interchanging those terms), and sometimes South Asian. But Brown? Never.

Somehow I thought I was different.

Brown - In high school that word was not as filled with ill intent. "You're not Black and you're definitely not white, so you're Brown," they'd say. A category simply to say I am lost somewhere in the middle of a Black-White universe.

Now, Brown has become an accusation.

I am not Black or white, I am evil.

How many times did white women look at me with clutched purses?

How many times did I hear whispers of "Muslim?"

How many times did I hear white men yell "Terrorist" from their American flag clad pickup trucks down Comm. Ave?

Mom says, "Make sure you tell people we are not like *those* people, like those Muslims."

You too, Ma?

"You know, Daddy put American flags in the car just so people know we *love* America!"

How many times had Daddy been called a terrorist for proudly wearing his namam on his forehead, dhoti around his waist and speaking with his accent around town? Was putting up a flag in every corner of the car as a sign of pride or a shield for protection, claiming, "We're one of the good guys! Gods bless America"?

My friend and I are talking as we walk across campus. I notice the amount of energy passersby are putting into avoiding eye-contact with us and yet peering at us with hyper-surveillance at the same time. Then, I saw the image that they were witnessing: Khadija wearing a hijab and me wearing baggy jeans and an oversized t-shirt.

Two Brown people, walking together.

Two terrorists, scheming an attack and being all things "unAmerican"

I could never truly imagine what her life has been for the last few days.

In a discussion section for class, we get to talking about current events. One kid starts to point to me, "Well if people like you didn't just kill innocent people or become suicide bombers... " I start to interrupt but soon realize that clarifying, "I'm not Muslim, I'm Hindu!" didn't make a difference to him. Most Americans didn't know the difference anyway. And distancing myself from being called a Muslim was worse. It made bare my own fear and complicity with Islamophobia, carried across oceans from the motherland. Bringing Partition of South Asia at the end of British colonial rule and decades of Hindu nationalism into this classroom, in the basement of the Psychology building. The world here did not care. Anyone not white would never be enough to be "American", even in Massachusetts where white Europeans came on a ship, killed Native people and created a world that we now call America. The irony.

I needed to do something. I began attending rallies against the war and racialization of Muslims, Sikhs and others, attended Friday evening prayers with my Muslim friends and even co-founded a group called Co-Exist, focused on interfaith awareness, dialogues and community building. It was my way of unlearning my own isms while leaning into what it meant to be Brown in the U.S. To be a perpetual foreigner, terrorist, model minority. The perfect wedge when needed by white powers to cause havoc on marginalized peoples.

Brown has become an accusation.

You are not Black or white, you are evil.

Brown has also allowed me to see how colonial fears were still clouding my view of the world. Brown has become an awareness, a commitment to being in community with my Brown siblings, learning, unlearning. Coloring Brown outside the lines that we are expected to inhabit.

32 READER'S STORY: WHAT DO YOU WISH TO SHARE WITH THE WORLD?

Dear Friend -

As you have read these pages, what has become clearer to you about your own story? What have you remembered about an important moment, person or place? What is a story that is uniquely yours that you wish to share with the world? Remember, if it's hard to write, it's probably worth writing about. No other being needs to see it if that's what you choose. Simply getting it out of your body liberates the Universe.

Take a deep breath and share your story:

33   ANCESTORS IN MY HANDS

I see my ancestors in my hands:
Brown, wrinkly, gleaming, strong yet soft.
A living map made of many generations, many sorrows, many
elations.
Outlining my family tree, as Ganga goes from the Himalayas
to the Samudra in veins across the land

Each line a proof of people who
lived,
      hoped,
            loved.
My great great grandmother
      My Muthajji
            My Ajji
                  My Amma
                     Me
Seems so simple as I stare at each crevice of my hand,

each bony finger
and each scar.
What scars do they wear?
What stories do they hold?

An incomprehensible morse code
communicating deep secrets,
passed down from
one   to the   other
a puzzle requiring careful study and patience to extract each
story.

Can they hear me?
What healing and holding are they manifesting at this
moment?

I remember my Ajji's hands.
Creased, not by age but years of creating life,
cooking, and caring for everyone else but herself.

Scars
        from handling wood stoves and coconut graters.
Softness
        from holding children and fresh flowers as she does her
morning prayers.
Hands that smell like a sweet mix of jasmine flowers, chilies
and sweat.

I feel my Amma's hands.

Displaying an intricate timeline of Celestial Bodies and
mapping her own hidden desires.
Each line
  thick and dark
  like lines of coffee
  drying in the Sun
  against the Brown Earth

Every now and then I am lucky to catch a whiff of my Ajji's
spirit
assembling dishes I've never tried before
but recipes intuitively
known in my veins
for as long as I have known anything in this world.

I can feel my mother's hands in mine
golden bangles dancing as she moves her hands back and forth
grating coconut flakes, like God making stars across the sky.

I see my Amma in my hands
Brown, wrinkly, gleaming, strong yet soft
A map made of many generations, many sorrows, and many
elations.

I see my ancestors in my hands
Brown, wrinkly, gleaming, strong yet soft
A living map made of many generations, many sorrows, many
elations,
Beyond my brown layer of skin,

not visible yet still deeply rooted are
my queer transcestors.

Each line a proof of people who
lived,
      hoped,
            loved.

Not connected by bloodlines
but by beauty,
      existence,
            visions
for a world where
we can all
be.
free.
Liberation through love.

Each line,
a lineage,
      a stream,
            a proclamation.
                    Our Queerness is Sacred,
Loving someone, a divine blessing.

How many of these saints can I see flowing in these palm
valleys?

      Urvashi
         James

Audre
Gloria
Mushtaq
Alexander
Michelangelo
Bayard
Terriel
Sten
Krishna
Shikandi
Ardhanareeshwara

Where are our other South Asian queer ancestors?
How many stories are
flowing through me
without a name?

I am now a root
A future ancestor in the making
Holding both my
Ajji and Audre
Rivers and Valleys
Ancestral Lands
Hopes and Visions
Sacred Mountains.
Bridges
between the world I know
and the magic I manifest.

My hands -

Vessels for visions
        Each touch is the
braiding
        of generations who have
built
        castles out of hope
and communities out of chaos.

                I see
            my ancestors
            in my hands.
Brown, wrinkly, gleaming, strong yet soft
A living map, branching out our role:
        Becoming the bridge.
    Between rivers and valleys
Between my Ajjis and all who are yet to come.

ROOTS AND ANCESTORS

34 A WALK WITH THAY

A flight to Paris,
a train to Bordeaux,
then another to Sainte Foy La Grande,
and a taxi ride into the hills of France.

I find myself entering Plum Village Monastery in south western France. This, the founding monastery of Thich Nhat Hanh, one of my spiritual teachers, has been on my list of places to visit for a long time. And since his recent passing, I knew my first visit to France would need to include a visit to the monastery, breathing in the air and sharing time with the monastics. I was only there for a few hours, but sometimes with the right medicine, just a little bit is enough.

I get out of the taxi and make my way to the office. The walk is beautiful with a grove of bamboo surrounded by a few buildings and various greenery. I am greeted by a monk who smiles as if we are long-time friends reconnecting. I first wander towards a building to my right, remove my shoes and enter a small meditation hall. I see a framed picture of Thay, a bowl of oranges and a beautiful wooden table holding an incense holder. I grab one of the sitting cushions lining the edge of the room and place it in front of the altar and light a fragrant incense stick and bow down, chanting:

"Om Shakya Munaye Bhudhaya". I plant the incense in the brass incense holder and get comfortable on the cushion as I enjoy some slow, deep breaths.

Breathing in, I know I am here
Breathing out, I can feel you here
Breathing in, I am grateful for this moment
Breathing out, what a wonderful moment
Breathing in, I have arrived
Breathing out, I am becoming my true self
Breathing in, I am enough
Breathing out, I am happy
Breathing in
Breathing out
In
Out
In
Out
In
Out
What an amazing feeling to
feel

the body just being.
Not trying, not doing, not thinking, just being.

After this short meditation, I bow down again and continue to wander the grounds. The little pond in the center of the main courtyard is mesmerizing with little water lilies, frogs, and a granite Buddha, with the gentlest smile, looking out at the miracle of this pond. Deep breaths. Around the corner, I see an open gazebo with a shelf full of teas, coffees, and mugs.

"Drink your tea, drink your clouds."

This is one of my favorite gathas, short meditation poems, which I find myself repeating with a cup of tea, especially when I'm on a plane staring out at a sea of clouds. So simple yet so profound. Each cup of tea is not just hot water and some leaves, but a truly miraculous manifestation of Universal elements that transform particles from water to steam to cloud, to rain as water that will nourish the land and my body.

Without the cloud, this tea would not exist
Without this tea, the clouds would not exist
In between these two is life.

Making tea is one of my favorite rituals because it forces me to slow down. Inviting reflection, attention to detail, and the ability to witness the transformation of clear, hot water interacting with tea leaves. A sacred dance in shades of brown.

I select a green jasmine tea bag (one of my favorites) and slowly pour hot water from the kettle into the cup. I still can't believe I'm actually here. How long have I dreamed of being able to be in Plum Village, on the ground where Thay (a word that means "teacher" and used by many people to refer to Thich Nhat Hanh) worked, lived, painted, and enjoyed so many cups of tea?. There were a couple of non-monastics milling around, since the monastery allows non-monastics to spend a few weeks on site. I wasn't feeling social so I spent some time by myself sitting in a beautiful chair, low to the ground, looking out at the Bell tower and the Great Hall, and painting mental images of all the beautiful greenery of this place. I slowly wander through the grounds, step by step-by-step, trying to move as *slowly* as possible, embracing each touch of my feet with the earth. I can hear Thay's words as if he was speaking them into my ear, "With each step, you kiss the Earth." Walking by the great hall, I could see some monks, meditating and cleaning up inside and I next get to the Bell Tower, a large gazebo with a huge metal bell side-ways and a large wooden paddle on rope that would be used to strike the bell at various times throughout the day to call for prayer and meditation. I can't understand much of the Viet-namese writing but there is one sign in English on one side of the roof that reads, "I have arrived. I am home." It's just beau-tiful: the red and gold paint against the wood.

Now, I meander along the edge of a large lily pond, covered in beautiful green lily pads and a handful of pink and white water lilies pushing through the water surface, and insects buzzing around.

"No mud, no lotus."
Life is not just about how pretty the lotus flower looks;
because the lotus flower cannot exist
without the mud and stagnant water from which it emerges.

Such a simple life lesson. When we are mired in the mess of our lives, it's easy to feel overwhelmed, yet when we can remember that only by going through the current situation can we have the life that we desire, it becomes a little bit easier to handle. My mother often says gold has to be put through an extreme heat source for it to become itself in all its glory and shininess.

I see the afternoon Sun dancing and reflecting along the water ripples, my own personal water show. I sit at a little bench at the edge of the pond, drinking my tea and imagining my teacher sitting next to me.

What would we have talked about?
What would we have learned about each other?
So much mud and so many lotuses.

I remember getting my first tattoo almost 15 years ago. It was early December in Los Angeles, which meant it was still beautiful weather. My friend Juhi lived in Westchester and we had been talking for a few weeks about getting tattoos, as both of us were going through major life transitions. She was going through a divorce and healing from various traumas and I was about to leave a job and go on a ship for four months. As an earth sign, (and someone that can't swim) I preferred seeing the water rather than being in the water so it was causing me a sea of anxiety.

Juhi and I had agreed to get our first tattoos together and one late Sunday morning we jumped in her blue Prius and started making our way around town to a list of tattoo shops that Google said were open. The first shop we went to was on La Cienega right in Westchester and they were open but had scheduled a day long tattoo session for someone doing a full sleeve. Eight hours on one arm sounds too painful. Tattoo shop number two was closed even though Google stated they would be open. Finally, we drove down Venice Boulevard to try one last shop. Juhi said, "If they are open, it's a sign that we should get it today. If not, we'll just wait for another day." The stars aligned and the shop was open and available! We walked into the tattoo shop looking like a comedy duo: a 50-something divorced, Indian woman and a 20-something Indian queer person wanting tattoos. I had ideas of what I wanted but was not yet sure what it would look like on my body. Juhi came ready with her vision; she wanted a bumblebee with the body drawn like a target so as to be a reminder to "bee here". A personal commitment to staying present to her journey of healing of trauma. I wanted something on my ankle to repre-sent groundedness as I was about to embark on a voyage around the world on a ship for four months and kinda freaking out about not feeling rooted on land.

Lotus flowers, like water lilies, grow in swampy waters. And the seeds are revered by many cultures, particularly in Asia because they represent beauty, perseverance and ancient wisdom. Lotus seeds can lay dormant in the Earth for about

250 years and if it rains they will sprout. How cool is that? So I picked a couple of different Lotus flower images and told the artist how I wanted them modified but gave him artistic license to make it happen. And within an hour, both of us had our first tattoos; we took our new bumble bee and budding lotus out to celebrate with a late lunch at our favorite Indian restaurant. Our friendship was not as resilient as the lotus. Our friendship ended a few years ago due to some misunderstanding and now I can't even remember what it was about. Juhi recently died without us having had any true reconciliation. Everytime I look at the lotus, it reminds me of that day when it felt like the whole world made sense and our friendship would be forever.

I come back to the bench in Plum Village, looking at the water lilies in the pond, bumble bees and dragonflies buzzing around, and sunlight sparkling on the water. How much of life is encapsulated in this little pond? The coexistence of insects and bugs and plants and water, and all the conditions for all of them to thrive. The water, the wind, the Sun, the spirit, the prayers, the bells, the suffering and the joy. I am overwhelmed with emotions and feel tears flowing down my cheek. It feels good to feel.

I bid goodbye to the lilies and dragonflies, and find myself meandering down a forest path, not really sure where I'm going. If the monks have been walking through these paths for decades, there has to be spiritual energies guiding me and they will not lead me astray. I love walking on forest trails with tall trees full of leaves. There's just something beautiful, calming and majestic about being in the middle of a grove of trees, like a hug from the Earth. In this forest path, the trees are made even more beautiful with gorgeous banners every fifty yards or so decorated with Thay's quotes and calligraphy.

> "I have arrived. I am home"
> "Joy is every step"
> "Walk like a Buddha"
> "This moment is full of wonders"
> "This is it"
> "I am in love with Mother Earth"
> "Be beautiful, Be yourself"

Taking time to stop at each sign, reciting it out loud and
taking a deep breath
Inhaling from the bottom of my toes
Exhaling to the top of the trees
As if breathing each step with Thay
As if tattooing the words from the banners and trees
into my spirit
into my bones
into my step

I arrive upon what has become my favorite part of the
monastery. Amongst the trees are several rows of Buddhas,
fifteen faces, in the same direction
looking over an open field.
Each, a slightly different posture.
Their expressions, serene.
Their features, precise yet delicate.

The Sun peeking through the branches
perfectly giving life to their features.

They are made up of a grayish black stone, and I find myself
taking interwoven paths between them. Taking time to study
each one's expression, hands, and the artistry of the robes that
look like actual fabrics. As I reach the end of the line, I find
myself sitting down, staring out at the open field, making
myself one of the stone Buddhas.

"There is a bodhisattva in all of us."

I pick up a fallen oak leaf and
place it in the palm
of one of the Buddhas.
An acorn in the palm of another.
Small offerings,
a reminder that
death and life
are simply concepts of
our consciousness.

The Buddhas and the stones that make them
are older than I can even comprehend,
yet this little leaf and acorn, recently
fallen from a tree.
I am
somewhere
in between these two.
I am everything,

I am nothing,
How beautiful.

What wisdom and universal messages do these Buddhas
carry?
What do they see when they look out on this open field?
How long have they been here?
How long will they be here?
Do any of these questions even matter?

I find myself singing
a favorite Carnatic ballad out loud,
"Marugelara, Oh Raghava!"
enjoying the echoing against the tree trunks
"Marugelara, Oooohh Ragavaaa..."
and the breeze adding a hum to my song like a choir.
Singing is healing in all seasons.
When I'm angry, sad, happy, lost, peaceful...
What a beautiful gift that we get to express all these
emotions,
and that we have planted within us
ways to cope with the various seasons of life.

Ding.

I hear the bell for lunch and walk to the dining hall, just
behind the bamboo grove in the main courtyard. A delicious vegetarian buffet of tofu, fresh veggies and brown
rice prepared with the harvest from the monastery's
gardens. In the tradition, we eat in silence. Noble

Silence. It's a time to not just eat, but to eat with intention.

Chew with intention.
Nourish with intention.

"With each bite, I offer gratitude."

Not simply scarfing down food but to actually pay attention to all the flavors and being in touch with how much work from the Sun, rain, gardener and cook has gone into making the meal. I wash my bowl and chopsticks. I take my shoes and sit on a rock by the small pond in the yard. A little bumble bee is whirling around me like a Dervish dancer in a trance.

"I have arrived. I am home."

Grateful for this afternoon, feeling Thay's presence and the many spirits who have walked this way. The taxi ride back is uneventful as I stare out the window. Chateaux, vineyards and farms roll by as we meander through the hillsides and little villages.

Everything is the same.
Everything is different.
I am
somewhere
in between these two.
I am everything.
I am nothing.

How beautiful?

Breathing in, I know I am here
Breathing out, I can feel you here
Breathing in, I am grateful for this moment
Breathing out, what a wonderful moment
Breathing in, I have arrived
Breathing out, I am becoming my true self
Breathing in, I am enough
Breathing out, I am happy
Breathing in
Breathing out
In
Out
In
Out
In
Out

What an amazing feeling to
feel!
The body just being.
Not trying, not doing, not thinking, but simply

being.

35   IF ONLY YOU KNEW

If only you knew...

That I still think of you
I call for you in the middle of the night
Like an elixir against my demons
Or an armor against the desert winds creeping under my
sheets

Or when I hear that one window that always creaks right
when I'm about to fall asleep

If only you knew how I yearn for your warm breath on the
base of my neck,
instantly melting me into your arms where I feel safe and
guarded.

Yearning for each inhale and exhale. The slightest wisp of

your beard adds a tingle to my soul as a universe unfolds
between my legs. Wiry chest hair brushing against my back,
like a soft wool sweater. your toes caressing my toes and your
arms clasping mine like they were created to be together, your
lips giving me life, like fresh rose petals on water.

My lover, my personal heater, my happiness in this moment. I
know you are not "mine". But your touch makes me surrender
to pleasure and I wonder how could I ever have felt at home
in anyone else's arms.

Is this lust? Is this love? Or simply a human desire for connection, for care, for comfort.

In the land of pleasure, words are but barriers to the heart.
Touch for touch,
breath for breath,
warmth for warmth.

I don't need you but I want you. For now this pillow will do.
In my dreams you are molded into me. Here. Right here.

If this damn window would just shut up,
I could be in your caress.

36 A EULOGY FOR MAMI

Señora LaRosa, or Mami as I called her, was our Spanish teacher, senior class advisor and the most spirited educator you'll ever meet. She died unexpectedly on June 15, 2007.

Dear Mami -

Frozen, I didn't believe it. I remember getting the phone call that you had died in your sleep. I had to call a few other people just to make sure it wasn't some terrible game of telephone gone wrong. How could you die? You were larger than life and always brought life into any room.

I heard your voice before I met you. You were singing at the top of your lungs in Spanish as gangly high schoolers walked by. The Salsa, Merengue or Bachata CDs playing loud enough to be heard down at the cafeteria! And of course you added your own lyrics to the beats. *"Hola! Vamos estudiantes! Es la hora de aprender!"* "Hello! Let's go students! It's time to learn!" As I turned the corner, there you were. Your voice was only outdone by the neon and sequined outfits accessorized perfectly with matching glasses of every color and shape. You looked like a rainbow of confidence in a sea of teenage angst. I didn't know so many bright colors could be contained in one outfit until I met you. I think I got my love of wearing colorful clothes from you.

I was a nerdy, socially awkward and shy kid in ninth grade, just trying to find my homeroom. You were joyful, loud and unabashedly in love with life. You were the spirit of the campus and could give any mascot/hype person in the world a run for their money.

You became Mami to me. I don't even remember when I started calling you that but you were the mother I needed in the most awkward phase of a young person's life: high school. It may have been around sophomore year when my homeroom was located just across the hallway from you and I would come to your room first to grab a piece of chocolate and dance a little salsa before school began. Though I had taken Spanish since sixth grade, I wasn't that good. But you insisted I speak in Spanish and would correct my grammar in a way that was clear but not shaming.

I was struggling to find "my people" in school. I had always been awkward and while I knew some kids in my class, I didn't really have friends. Growing up in my orthodox, immigrant family, I was told having friends was a distraction I couldn't afford and that putting my head down into my books and making my parents proud were my only objectives in life.

To their dismay, I fell in love with a Puerto Rican boy who happened to be in Alianza Latina, a group on campus to celebrate Latine culture. He was a Junior while I was just a Freshman at the high school. During a schoolwide assembly, he and others performed some cool dance moves and invited people to join the club, noting that, "You don't have to be Latino! Just come, dance, learn about our culture and have some fun!" I couldn't wait to join so I could get to know him better. Nothing would come of that infatuation with a straight boy but catalyzed our relationship as I got to know you as a friend and mentor, seeing as you were the group's advisor.

I had joined a few clubs but it was after joining Alianza Latina that my transformation began. I was a nervous wreck going to my first meeting but I enjoyed hearing people talking about being proud of their culture and wanting to find ways to support their community on campus and in our town. While there were a handful of Indian and other South Asian peers, I didn't find much in common with them seeing as I was not a child of doctors or engineers, didn't live in the fancy part of town, nor did I play tennis or take fancy vacations. I was a working class immigrant and found that I had more in common with Latine and Afro-Caribbean folks who were part of the club than with any South Asian peers. I was enjoying getting to know more about Latine culture, especially Puerto Rican food and music. Slowly, I began to speak up in meetings and get more involved, volunteering to set up or take photography to make sure we were archiving the work and had sufficient images for the year book. I attended every event possible, from city parades to potlucks in someone's backyard. After Hurricane George and Irene, we raised funds and collected donations of blankets and canned goods to provide direct aid for communities in Puerto Rico, Cuba and Mexico. We collected everything from aluminum can tabs to eyeglasses to be repurposed for folks in developing countries. I spent hours observing you, Mami, and the way you built community. You were always there to support individual students with a closet full of snacks and advocated along with marginalized people around campus policies or access to resources. You have given me several gifts that have transformed my life.

The gift of service. I was always amazed by the stories you would share after each summer spent in a garbage dump in Tijuana. There are still dozens of little girls named Christina in your honor in that community of garbage rumagers. You would eat what they ate, sleep where they slept and fundraise to get a van so you could take the children to see magical things like the ocean or learn how to use more hygienic toilets you had just helped build.

The gift of travel. I knew nothing of the world beyond visiting family in India and living in the U.S. until my junior year when you took a few students to Ecuador as part of an exchange program you had established. I was too afraid to even imagine going since I knew my family couldn't afford such luxuries but you calmed me down and helped all of us fundraise the heck out of every possible bake sale and volunteering event, teaching us to save up so we could make the trip happen. I remember you surprised us all with a limo from the high school to the airport! We felt so special, a group of mostly Black and Brown, middle and working class kids, traveling to another country! We took classes at the international school, stayed with local families, and learned about local indigenous arts.

The gift of a chosen family. Somehow along the way, you also convinced me, the awkward skinny Brown kid with no athletic ability, to be the Blue Dragon - the high school mascot. From a million bake sales in front of local grocery stores to football games, I learned that putting on the costume helped me shed some of my own masks and accept myself for who I am. When I was nervous about coming out to you about my sexuality, I lied and said I was interested in a girl at school. You didn't mock or question my words, but just affirmed me. Then, a few days later accepted me when I came out to you - the first adult I had ever come out to (looking back I realize how transparently queer I was, but I really thought I was doing a good job of "hiding it" and playing a heterosexual). That was such an important moment to help me realize that my queerness is not a disease but a divine gift. I remember talking about how scared I was about telling my family and without hesitation, your response was "If you ever need a place to stay, this is your home! That room is for you!" Just knowing you and your family were there helped me get through some of my darkest days. Realizing I could have a birth family while also cultivating a chosen family has been such a source of healing in my life.

Mami, I miss you every day and am grateful for all the lessons

I've learned. I cannot imagine where I would be without you. I remember you once reciting words of Rumi:

"Deja de actuar tan pequeño. Tu eres el universo en movimiento estático."
"Stop acting so small. You are the Universe in ecstatic motion."

I think of that moment whenever I'm scared. I remember you had a photo of a red octagonal street sign that read, "Stop and smell the roses" just outside of your classroom. I loved that sign. Now every time I see a rose, I have to stop and smell and think of you. Thank you for being such an integral part of my becoming. Thank you for being my guide in the dark when I did not know if light existed. *Gracias por todo.*

Abrazos -

Raja, tu hije

MOON ROSE

37 RADICAL SURRENDER TO PLEASURE

After hours of crying, I am curled into a ball on the cool wooden floor of the now empty living room, wishing I could just disappear. Dark, naked, weary brown skin against the glistening grains of oak, like a wounded animal forgotten in a field of dry grass. Who knew the living room would be the site of a sort of death of someone I should be rather than who I am? *Chandamama*, the full Moon streaming into the room through the open patio doors, covering me in a sense of ancestral care as if to say, "We got you. Now, let go!"

How do I let go?

How do I let go of everything I had been taught to work towards until this point? I had the fancy title at a fancy campus with a fancy salary, living in a fancy condo, and an immigrant family friendly and practical car (a Honda) that was paid off. I had finished my doctorate, and possessed everything that I thought would make me happy. And I was miserable. Throughout my professional career, dozens of mentors and friends have pushed me to want "the next best thing" or "moving on up" in higher education administration. I've been in education my whole damn career. I was built for this, trained for this, have three degrees for this... but I could see that there were some shenanigans on campus and I was being used as a pawn for political games beyond my purview. I had to figure out if I'd rather be unemployed than put up with a person who psychologically abused me almost daily just to keep my job that looked good on paper but in real life came with monsters that were unraveling my life and dignity.

Seeing that I had no safe way out of this political warfare, I left a job that was so harmful it almost killed me. My health was out of whack and my doctor was worried about my test results and I was worried about my sanity. I had been holding on to so much pain. Some endured by me and others caused by me. How do I recover from what feels like the lowest point of my life? It's like watching my own funeral, painful yet I couldn't look away. Just moments ago I was considering "What if I didn't exist?", "Would the world be better or worse?" and "Is this what life is supposed to feel like all the time?" The Universe was speechless to my queries. I made a pact that night that has transformed my life in every way possible.

This is my radical surrender to pleasure, myself and the Universe.

I let go.

I let go of my "vision" for what I was supposed to do with my life. What title I was supposed to hold and what lifestyle I was supposed to pursue.

Am I becoming a *Sanyaasi?* A monk?... maybe?

Condo leased out to a friend, car neatly parked in a friend's driveway and all my new material symbols of this new life given away.

Beds, gone.

Dining set, gone (except for two funky chairs I put in storage and hoping they will go with my next dining set... if I ever get another one).

Three couches, gone (including a custom made, peacock blue velvet couch that cost wayyyy too much money but made me happy for the months I got enjoy it).

Art... oh so much art, all bubble wrapped and neatly packed into boxes for storage.

CD's, DVD's (yes, I'm *that* old), books and decor along with the five bookshelves that housed them, gone.

My ego and career-centered life for the last fifteen years, along with most of my suits and winter clothes, packed up and donated to the non-profit thrift store up the road.

Several friends have offered to create positions or give me some temporary work so that I have a job. I decline and put those in a box and give them away as well.

Two wooden U-Haul storage pods with the ugly vinyl orange cover are dropped off in the backyard on a rainy Tuesday.

The next morning, movers are laughing.

There are not enough contents in the large black and yellow tupperware containers of scarves, cardboard boxes of kitchenware and books and a whole box full of family pictures from the 80's onwards to fill even three-quarters of one pod, let alone two.

Wednesday evening the pod is taken to storage.

And I find myself considering dark thoughts while staring at the night sky with dried tear stains across my cheeks, mimicking the marks I see on the Moon.

Up to this moment, my prayers with the Gods have been about asking for this thing or bartering for another professional achievement. I will pray to you if you do this in my life. Or I will donate my weight's worth of sugar if you help me get a good grade on this exam, etc. Rather than asking what I want, I stop putting boundaries on your vision and just say I will follow.

I will follow.
I will follow.
I will follow.

I trust you, *Chandamama*. I follow where you lead me. No questions, no requests.

Just walking.
Guide me.
I surrender.
I surrender.
I surrender.
I surrender to pleasure, myself and the Universe.

Ancestor Audre Lorde says, "We tend to think of the erotic as an easy, tantalizing sexual arousal. I speak of the erotic as the deepest life force, a force which moves us toward living in a fundamental way." Seeing my sense of pleasure as not just sexual but the "deepest life force" that guides me to my greatest self. Not titles or cars or homes, but a force that transforms us from seeking things to being the force of life.

I surrender.

Adrienne Maree Brown decrees, "Pleasure is the point. Feeling good is not frivolous, it is freedom." My pleasure is not just about feeling good, it's about liberation and justice from systems that would rather have me in a job that was killing me than in the world, taking in all the beauty.

I surrender.

Marie Kondo promotes a way of living where only things that bring us joy deserve to be in our living space. I interpret it a bit broader to focus on building better boundaries and making space only for people, places and even things that bring me joy. Learning to let go of clothes and homes hasn't been too terrible though letting go of people has been harder than I expected. Yet making time and space for people who continue to harm or take advantage of me is not conducive to my liberation.

I surrender.

The Hindu Scriptures pronounce *"Aham Brahmasmi"* "I am the Divine." I am made of the same elements as the Gods and therefore what is good for me is good for the Universe. And adding on Lama Rod Owen's belief that we must live in pleasure but not get stuck to its pursuit. "To love my pleasure is not the same as being attached to my pleasure. Loving pleasure means that I allow it to be itself. I enjoy when it arises and I let it go when it leaves. When we are in relationship with our pleasure in this way, then it can direct us into the experience of spaciousness, and that spaciousness is the basis of happiness, joy and bliss." Does the ability to just follow this unseeable force mean I am staying present or I am just taking silly risks or chasing pleasure? I mean why let go of a job that has given my family so much pride, even though they don't fully understand what I actually do? Should I feel guilty for taking such a jump and turning down perfectly good job offers? No guilt, no silly risks. Surrendering to pleasure without needing or desiring it, like an addiction, is how we can cultivate a radical surrender to pleasure.

I surrender.

bell hooks states, "Our freedom is sweet. It will be sweeter when we are all free." So how can we embrace a radical surrender to pleasure that helps others do the same. Living in pleasure. Teaching in pleasure. Eating in pleasure. Being in pleasure. Loving in pleasure.

I surrender.

Gratitude not Guilt. I am grateful for a situation where I know I am financially able to take care of myself for over a year if need be. My head fought hard to make me take any of the roles offered to me for the sake of our family's financial security (my immigrant parents' highest expectation for me), while my heart wins over, recognizing that I don't need a job right now to support them or nourish myself. I can be grateful without feeling guilty that this is the choice. Even at this moment, I am not looking to survive, I'm looking to live.

I surrender.

Next morning, I pack up a few clothes, books and my shattered spirit into a carry-on suitcase - essentials for what I thought would be a ten-day trip to Cuba but became the blueprint for more than four years of wandering around the world, radically surrendering to pleasure. I can taste the late summer air, full of a sweetness of blooming leaves mixed with sweltering tar and my own sweat.

I let go. I follow. I surrender. I experience freedom.

38 11:11

11:11
A sacred number
               A sad moment
Since your death I see
        I see this number everywhere
On the clock
               On my phone
                       On a billboard
                               Even in my dreams
Why is it that I think of you more now
        than when you were alive?
You were too young,
               too strong,
too healthy
               to die at forty eight.
        Or so I thought.
Your death

has given me a million reminders of my life.

An ability to
    be present
        to see the wonder
            of this wild thing called life.
Now everytime I see
    11:11
I breathe.
    I dream.
        I savor.
            I live.
You along with so many that are no longer in this earthly
body
Like divine messengers reminding me of the preciousness of
life.

Each breath
    Each second
        Each day
            Each year
                Each life
Each day, a birthday,
a reminder of the miracle of life.

No guarantees. No coincidences.

By living our lives
Squeezing all
    the laughter,

tears,
    samosas,
        nature walks,
            bear hugs,
                broken hearts,
                    wine tastings,
                        Tarot readings,
                            meditations,
                                pillow fights,
and every moment of living this dream.

We get to make magic.
Transforming
    Oxygen into
        Breath into
            Body into
                Action into
                    Dreams into
                        this thing called Life.
I live for the life, blooming in all its awkwardness, joy and sorrow.
11:11 just adds a reminder that in the best and worst moments
We still have a breath

Truly messy and all over the place.
I don't control life nor does life control me.
We are in a divine dance, a tango for two.
A perfect reflection.
    Life : Living

Joy : Joying
Pain : Paining
Death : Dying

11 : 11

Now I know that
Each moment
    I breathe
      I dream
        I savor
          I live
            is sacred.

No guarantees. No coincidences.
Sacred.

39 COMING OUT IN THE LAUNDRY ROOM

In my family, coming out is not a one time act. It has to be done regularly or they forget.

Dear Mummy -

We were so close at one time. It's sad to see where we are now. Everything changed when I came out and I haven't been able to see a way for our paths to converge again.

First, I came out to you when I was 17 in high school. We talked about the various Queer gods of Hindu mythology and how I hoped for a love like those someday. You brushed it off saying that mythology and reality cannot be the same yet I could see in your eyes a confirmation of a truth you have known for many years.

Next, I came out to you in my early 20s during college. When I refused to go through with an arranged marriage to a woman

I did not know, and I could not love. You called me selfish and said that I had broken your word and your trust. "Marriage is not about love" you said, "Maybe this woman can 'fix' you."

For my twenty sixth birthday, you visited for six weeks. Within four days of us cohabitating in a one bedroom apartment, shingles manifested on my body as if trying to protect me from your anger. Through the pain, I took you to dinner with my friends to meet a group of Queer South Asian and family members. I came out to you in the car and wanted you to know I have a strong community. You said, "Oh they are nice people, just *not our kind of people*. You need some new friends". Then you were silent all the way home. We spent a weekend with my boyfriend wandering the parks of San Francisco. You were friendly enough, as if meeting someone next to you on a plane - an inconvenience. "He's a nice boy," you said, "but you shouldn't be so friendly with boys *like that*. It is not our culture."

In my early 30s, I would call to say hello. Why could you never call me? "Oh, You know I'm just so busy. It's easier for you to call. It's not like you have a family or anything." You would take every chance to cut me down. A tongue sharper than a sword. I tell you about my research and work supporting LGBTQ youth and addressing HIV stigma and you respond with, "Why do you waste your time on this dirty stuff? You should have become a doctor to make us proud." I push back, "This is my community, these are people with lives, stories, and so much to offer the world. I am queer and these are my people and this is the research that will help me get my doctorate." You pierce my spirit with a comeback, "Oh but you won't be a *real* doctor."

At 35 years old, I bring you and Daddy over to my apartment in Culver City. You like that I live on Jasmine Avenue. "A very nice street name," you say. My small apartment has Queer, Hindu and Queer Hindu art and books strewn across various surfaces because I was not about to change home to hide myself from you. Daddy takes a nap after lunch and I go to the laundry room at the other end of the building. I'm starting a mixed load wash cycle when you corner me by standing in the doorway. Thank goodness I am not claustrophobic.

"Kelsa hage nadithaaidhe?" "How's work going?"

I'm surprised, so it takes me a few seconds to respond to you.

"Chanagidhe" "It's going well."

You've never been interested in my work as an LGBTQ center director. "We have some new student groups. One of them is actually a South Asian LGBTQ organization and it's been wonderful to coach them. And my research and teaching is great! I have interviews for my research with Indian LGBTQ students and the course on HIV is going really well. The students are bringing so much to the readings and discussions!"

"Why is everything the gay with you? Why do you support them? It's not good. You should be normal. Marry a nice girl and make us happy."

"Ma. Are we really gonna have this conversation again?! I am gay. I am queer. I love my work and teaching. I am 'normal', whatever that means, but I'm not interested in marrying a woman. I want to be with a man (I decided not to add a layer about having cis and trans polyamorous partners to the conversation if we couldn't even get the basics down). I want to be happy."

"What does marriage have to do with happy? Life is just life. People keep asking me why you're not married and I don't know what to say. Such a waste of bringing you here to the states and this education. We should have just left you in India and you would not be speaking all this nonsense now."

"Well, you did bring me here and gave me access to the education that has given me a sense of who I am and how I want to show up in the world. So really it's your fault that I'm as queer as I am. I think you're also forgetting that I get my stubbornness from you."

I move the laundry into the dryer and find the low humming to be calming while you are still conducting your inquisition.

"You know there are some young women in India who have been widowed so at least you could marry them. Just leave them there and you'll have a wife and do whatever or whoever you want to do."

"What?! While I appreciate the progressiveness of you being okay with having a daughter-in-law that has been a widow, I think you've missed the point I've been making for twenty years... . I'm GAY. Like, I'm the queerest unicorn around. Have you seriously forgotten how many times we repeat this cycle?!"

"I just want you to be happy... "

"No, you're not worried about my happiness, you're just worried about *your* happiness. I get it. You want me to be 'settled'. Guess what? I am settled, I have a great career, love my research, I make enough to take care of you and the family back home and most of all, I'm queerly happy!"

How many times do I have to come out to you for you to understand that I am not broken or lost?

After all these years, I'm still not sure if you fully understand who I am, and who I love. We have missed out on so many important milestones in each other's lives simply because it was easier for me to stay away than be subject to playing a role that fits within your narrative, and I can't get those back. I have tried, time and time again, to figure out how to have a relationship where we can be in each other's lives, and still feel affirmed and loved for who we are. I'm tired, Ma, I'm tired of having to prove myself. Of having to prove that I am worthy of being who I am. I gave up on wanting your approval a long time ago, but it still stings every now and then. And I know life hasn't been easy for you either. Nowadays, our phone calls are even rarer, given your hearing loss and stubbornness. While I learned to never expect an "I love you" from the other side of the phone, since that's never been part of our culture, I would love to know you again. I know changing cultural values is not like simply changing a load of laundry, and yet I continue to hope that someday you will allow yourself the time to call and talk about who we have become.

Your child -

Raja

40 A PLACE OF RESPITE

Breathing in... breathing out
Life, like waves, constantly moving

Samudra Devi - Ocean Spirit
I rest upon a driftwood, the shape of a wrangled candy cane.
Tan, brown washed out yet laden with memories of a
previous life. Now resting peacefully on the sea shore. What
stories are ingrained within you, my friend?

I touch the cream and rose colored grainy sand nestled in
between my toes. An almost tickling feeling but warmer. I
never cease to be amazed at how gently the sand adjusts to
the shape of my feet and fills every little wrinkle and curve.

Handfuls of these seaside gems land upon my feet with each
wave, as if a highly potent cement binds me
to this exact moment,

a gentle respite from a heavy and confusing world.

Each grain carries a story of
a once-upon-a-time mountain who now exists in pieces,
spread across oceans and shores.
Life is like this.
One moment, a mountain.
Another moment, a grain of sand.
What beautiful simplicity.

Once a mountain... now a grain.

I rise, a bit wobbly as my feet carry the weight of my body and
baggage, sinking deeper into the sand's caress. Did you know
we use two-hundred muscles to take a single step?

Beginning my journey to touch the sea,
each step on the sand becomes a monumental achievement.

I wonder how many muscles we use to love?

From the driftwood to the water,
each step getting softer, less filled with debris and
more filled with heavier, wetter sand.

I can feel the softness of wet sand.

Does the sand prefer to be dry by the driftwood or wet under
the crashing wave?
Now I feel the

cool frothy water slide
against my feet, bringing an ancestral smile
with no effort at all.
And when the water draws away,
my feet sink deeper into the sand
a new valley around my ankles

Sliding forward... drawing away.

Open palms facing the sparkly ocean
with a vast network of waves and reflections
creating a
magical kaleidoscope
like an interactive puzzle of emotions colliding,
coexisting and complementing.

The breeze whizzes softly through my fingertips,
Anointed
A fine layer of salty ocean mist kisses my skin, as if to say,
"You are home now *Kanda*, you are here."

Breathing in... breathing out

With each breath,
the
salty air
enters deep into my
chest

I find myself offering a small prayer:

May the salt in our food nourishe us
May the salt in the ocean heal us
May the salt in our tears liberate us

A simple verse, a conversation with Samudra Devi,
an offering for life

I gather salt from the sea
I return salt to the sea
A cycle of life, death and all the meandering journeys in
between.

I sit in the water, allowing it to cover me,
feeling little zings of life
as salt water touches some unhealed wounds on my skin,
reminding me
I am a work in progress.

This.
This place will always
be
my respite from the world,
from myself.

Driftwood, sand, ocean, breath, breeze, Sun, healing, caress.

Everything when done with heart, is prayer.

YOU ARE HOME

41   A LETTER TO MY FUTURE SELF

Dear Beloved,

Here are some musings that keep me up at night. I write this letter not as an oracle nor with a list of desires for what I hope will have happened in the future, but simply as a bridge to where we have been and where we find ourselves now. This book is really just for you; a chronicle of moments, missteps and meanderings through the last four decades. I don't know how many more I have by the time I get to you but I send this into the universe as an invitation of sorts. Each word is a star trying to figure out its own significance in the larger galaxy of being. There are so many stories I could have told on these pages but some are not yet ready to be brought to light, while others are just fuzzy memories not worth remembering yet still a part of the cosmic debris we leave behind. I am extremely proud of still being here. Against all odds and barriers, we have breathed new life into each day, living, struggling, loving, creating, and flowing. For a long time, I have tried and tried to make myself feel a sense of belonging in various contexts because I thought that's what I was supposed to do. Somewhere, I had internalized an expectation that the goal of life is to belong to someone, to somewhere, to some space, to some community, or to some exciting job title. But, the older I get, the more I realize that belonging may not be possible for some people. Now, that doesn't mean I don't feel at home anywhere or that I don't have people who I consider "my people". But, I'm truly not sure if the immigrant queer Brown experience allows for one to ever feel a true sense of belonging, whatever that is, especially in this country and at this time.

"The wound is where the light enters." – Rumi

I've had several friends tell me that they regularly play a game of "Where in the world is Raja?" and often express their envy at my current life of living out of a carry-on suitcase. "Oh, it must be so fun to travel so much and live your life!" they say. Yes, I am so grateful that I get to live this fabulous life that I had always envisioned yet never thought possible for me. This wandering is not just fun but has been critical to my own healing these last five years. Truth be told, many times, it's not that glitzy; it's actually quite lonely and scary. Growing up in a home that told me my skin is too dark and my queerness is too much, I have spent my life hiding and trying to be just enough to belong. Just Queer enough to not be too much, just Brown enough to not be too American and just American enough to not be seen as "one of those immigrants". How much fear do we enmesh into our flesh and how much of our soul gets entangled within the muscles and bones of expectations and trauma? Is this how all marginalized people feel at all moments?

My spoken English accent often meets greetings of, "Oh you don't sound Indian at all!" What does that even mean? I was born in India and have Indian ancestry and therefore I am Indian. Indian enough. And regardless of my accent, I am who I am. As I think back on my education, my first experience in U.S. public schools was being put back a grade with no offer of ESL classes because some administrator decided I was not fluent in English. My language learning curve was equated to a lack of intelligence, disregarding the impact of moving across the world to live with people I barely knew or fighting shadows I had yet to face. Unknowingly, this experience drove me to peel away my accent - one word, one intonation, one self-hating moment at a time. I wonder how my life would have constellated had I retained my "Indian" accent. And now, I get annoyed when my Indianness is questioned because of my accent and yet being reminded I'm not American because of my skin color.

What do we lose when we move from our motherland?
What do we hold on to when we stay?
What do we do when we have no agency in these choices?
What do we gain when we go beyond familiar waters?
What wounds are deep enough to be carried across oceans and lifetimes?
What is my healing? What is our healing?

Oh, Ancestors and Guides, what is this wound where the light can enter? What is this light I am awaiting? What is the light I am holding? This world feels so hard and broken all around me and the light is flooding in through the wound, making it unbearable sometimes and yet, the light makes way for clarity and consciousness. Birds awaken me from my slumber of self-pity with their cheerful chirping. Political divides that feel unrepairable and people that are wounded need us to lead the way. Though salty water can kill most plants, my tears have nourished me into being and have deeply rooted my healing journey in the soil of my skin. Light makes way for roots to take hold in my soul.

Stuck.

Whiteness prized and pursued with billion-dollar markets of bleaching creams and self-hate.
Blackness dehumanized and murdered without care.
Browness made relevant only when convenient to justify divisiveness or war.

Brown.
Stuck.
In between.
Not enough of one and too much of another.
Yet, invisible and messy within this incongruent American racial equation.

When innocent Black people are reprimanded or killed, as if they are simply target practice for a system built to destroy them, has our world become nothing but a violent video game, virtual/reality becoming blurred? When a white life is deemed worth saving, even when that person is caught red-handed with bloody gun prints, they are somehow allowed to live. Yet, Black and Brown and Immigrant people sitting in a car or eating at a bar or simply speaking a language with an accent deemed "un-American" marks them as a terrorist threat.

When politicians simply use "us" and "them", as if some people are evil just because they think differently while both parties continue to fund displacement and destruction of innocent civilians halfway around the world and right here on our streets, so that some white man's pockets get bigger with bloody black tar. What is a vote if we are only sold the hope of a mediocre lesser evil? Those already living in the margins making more concessions to expand the margin yet still stuck in their stagnant life context without the luxury of having American Dreams.

Why are there hungry mouths begging for food in the richest country in the world that spends more money and time meddling with other parts of the world than taking care of our own? Why can't we figure out a healthcare system that actually cares for our health? It feels like the purpose of these systems is to ensure the bottom line rather than preventing a patient's flatlining.

When will we as Asian Americans recognize how colonial mindsets still drive some of our desire for White-adjacent aspirations? Given the horrific attack against Asian Americans over the history of this nation, and specifically in Atlanta just a few years ago, and the growth of AAPI voting and political engagement, how are we as a community voting towards our collective liberation? What are the intersecting identities and factors that influence our voting patterns and where we have work to do to help our community understand the deep impact of voting for candidates that won't support our causes and realities. Especially as there are large and complicated economic and immigration gaps within the AAPI voting bloc, and recognizing the ways we have and continue to be both used as a wedge while being made invisible of our impact and needs, within the White-Black framework of politics. How can we not buy into being the wedge but lean into being a fulcrum of social change?

There are several Hindu scriptures and rituals where we end with "May this offering liberate my ancestors". May my own healing liberate my ancestors. There is so much light in the world, even in the darkest moments. During a recent psychedelic healing journey, I found myself in a fetal position, fully covered in a blanket and having an out of body experience of feeling tingles all through my body and noticing how strange it all feels as if looking through a window into someone else's life. Speaking to my mother from the womb and seeing ancient serpents, goddesses of fertility and transformation, guiding me back to myself. A few minutes later I found myself in the bathroom, peeing and crying. Feeling my anger leaving my body as I speak words of forgiveness to a father I've never known yet have carried with me for far too long. Looking in the mirror and splashing off the tears on my face with cool water; releasing years of self-doubt and self-hatred.

And a poem emerges:
I am rooted. I am a tree. In the desert. I am free.
I am rooted. I am free. In the desert. I am a tree.
I am the root. I am the desert. I am the tree. I am free.

I am the light and the darkness.

What does it mean to be the both/and? When we are the harmed and the harmer. Just in different contexts. I know my imperfections and I'm grateful for the ways I am humbled in this life. And remembering my own growth. What is it that we are on this Earth to accomplish? To learn to be more human? To make a difference? To strive? To struggle? Simply, to be?

I do not believe in coincidences.

Wound
Ancestor
Light
Future
Darkness
Healing
Living.

My life has been defined by death. Death of loved ones, leading to a painful life lesson or a transformative change in circumstance, giving me a life I could never have imagined. How intricately life and death are interwoven into our paths! What do I desire of you? A life of living into pleasure, health and community, with no regrets. I wish you a love that deserves all the love I have to give. I wish you a life where each sunrise inspires a smile and each sunset invites gratitude.

How lucky are we to be alive? Even on the hardest days, we have simple gratitudes all around us. A little yellow flower growing through the cement sidewalk or a child jumping in a puddle or a meal that tingles every cell of the body. Amidst the wars and woes, we can choose compassion and trust. You are here for a reason. At this moment. In this space. We don't have to know why yet, but the Universe will open pathways when we are ready. In the end, it's comforting to know my life is but a quick blip in the Universal arc of time. Perfection is overrated and pleasure is underrated. I love that you love hard, without abandon. Don't lose that spirit. Love because it feels good even if pain is inevitable. It makes life worth living. Breathe and touch the Earth with your feet. Let the grass and dirt caress your toes and thoughts. Know that the stars are always there, even when we can't see them. We can always feel them.

Will I have forgiven myself yet for being imperfect?
Will my heart still be loving in the face of adversity and loss?
Will our humanity find its way to eradicating human war and violence?
Am I still finding joy watching a butterfly flutter around?

Will I have stopped finding the flaws as I stare at the mirror
and just embrace the miracle that is my body?
Will our systems be capable of rewiring themselves to meet
the needs of our communities?
Will we center the marginalized people in our healing work?
Will my friends and I live in a commune together, as an
eccentric gathering of visionaries?
What new world are we birthing with each breath and each
word?

Our lives are stars stretched on a canvas of hope and histories.
Divine messages of mattering.
Filling the wound with stories, connections and hope.
Light that transforms wounds into scars.
Scars into stars.
Stars into chaos.
Chaos into constellations.

<3

A hopeful me.

42 DRAGONFLY ON THE RUNWAY

Dragonfly on the runway
Metal birds slowly awaken as the Sun peeks through the
clouds
painting the sky with pinks, oranges and blues.
Whizzing by,
a dragonfly,
eager and triumphant. Excited for the day and curious about
her surrounding scene.
Somehow she has found herself on the tarmac
Surrounded by other much larger dragonflies, just a bit boring
in color and not as flexible.
Cold, buzzing and shiny
Full of people and things, these metal cousins are mighty
yet yearn to be the dragonfly:
Swift, colorful and free to roam without limit
Dragonfly on the runway

I am rooted, I am a tree.
In the desert, I am free.

I am rooted, I am free.
In the desert, I am a tree.

I am rooted. I am a tree.
In the desert. I am free.

I am rooted. I am free.
In the desert. I am a tree.

43   BEING A BEING (A PRAYER)

Each time I sit
a prayer, a breath, a reminder
    of life,   of death.

Each in-breath a new day, a new set of connections within my
cellular body.
Each out-breath a new release of toxins, beliefs or words that
do not serve me.

As the Moon follows the Sun and Sun follows the Moon, my
breath moves in tune to a natural rhythm, guided by my heart:
a miracle.

What is a heart but a divine imagination for joy?
Each breath a new day.
And a brain, a devout pilgrim?

Conspiring together to bring me home to my true self.
To my

peace.

My own galaxy with a personalized Moon and Sun, moving
together with ease as if it is the most intuitive way of being.
One that exists beyond time, space and desire. A being.

A noun and a verb. A miracle. Being. Be-ing.

Stri and Purusha, Feminine and Masculine. And every Being
infinitely bridging the two.

Conspiring together to bring me home to my true self.
To my

peace.

How two become one:

Life and Death,
Inhale and Exhale,
Sun and Moon,
Heart and Brain,
Stri and Purusha,
Being and Being.

They are not opposites. Nay they are the same. There is no
Life and Death. Only

Life-Death. A bridge called being.

With every moment of life we are reminded of the inevitability of death.

With every witnessing of death we are reminded of the abundance of life.

Life-Death
Inhale-Exhale
Sun-Moon
Heart-Brain
Stri-Purusha
Be-ing

Being is the bridge.

Being divine pilgrims on a journey to ourselves. The Journey and Destination.

Journey-Destination.

Being.

Each time I sit, a prayer, a breath, a reminder of being.

EPILOGUE

As I write this page, I am in northern Minnesota with dear friends in their lodge home, overlooking a large span of grass with heaps of melting snow on a warmer than usual January day. What a full-circle moment to write this in Prince's home state who inspired the tag line for this book with his musical genius and fabulous sense of style and self-assuredness. Everytime I'm in the MSP airport, I can't help but wander through the store dedicated to Prince's music and memorabilia and it reminds me of the power of artists to change our world for the better with each thoughtful word, musical note or brush stroke.

Just this week, Minnesota adopted a new flag design for the state, going from a flag of many colors adorned with a colonial image of a European farmer tilling land while an Indigenous person rides on a horse as if being shunned into the wilderness while the land is tamed by the new Minnesotans. As if the only way to live in this land is to control it rather than living in harmony with it. The new flag features a darker shade of blue in an abstract shape of the state alongside a lighter blue that completes the rectangle representing all the water that makes the land of 10,000 lakes a blue paradise. In the middle of the abstract state design lies an eight pointed star, paying homage to being the North Star state - a symbol of stability and direction. While many stars in space swim around and change positions based on season, the North Star continues to be an anchor for seafarers and dreamers alike, a constant reference point to calculate all other interstellar movements across the night sky. I like the simplicity of this new flag - an attempt to correct racist imagery that has been around too long and aspires to a new image of a state that has struggled between becoming a safe haven to one of the largest Southeast Asian and African immigrant refugee populations in the country to a community still trying to make sense of a Black man's murder by police violence just a few years ago. George Floyd's death led to one of the most powerful movements of communal reckoning with racist history, oppressive systems and cultural values that continue to harm and disempower marginalized communities. What does it mean to honor the past while repositioning our path to a future of liberation for all? How do we honor the North Star of our values while adjusting our galactic maps to constellate new beings?

Of course there are some people in this state that feel the flag is a "liberal attack" on the state's history and want to preserve the past yet if we stay focused on making things great again, we simply retreat to worlds that were not great for a majority of people in the world. In writing this book, I've learned that while there are an infinite catalog of stories and life happenings, some stories are not worth preserving, especially if they have and continue to cause harm to myself or others. One story I considered writing was about someone who caused me great harm as a supervisor but including that letter in this collection felt like it actually memorializes that person into my story forever. While writing them a letter was healing, there is no need for this person to take up precious space in this constellation of my life. I burned the letter and released it into the Universe.

Writing is a radical act, especially when the author is positioned in what Gloria Anzaldúa calls the Borderlands/Las Fronteras, a space of both/and and neither, all at once. What does it mean to constellate my story with my own words and worlds? And to queer the process of constellating by various storytelling strategies? While we were having dinner, a new friend asked why I am writing a book. The first thought in my head was that this book is about leaving a legacy, but I realize that such a vision makes this whole process of writing a book about the future while the stories keep us in the past. All while missing a critical moment, the present. In reflecting and writing I have created potential and you as the reader have given it meaning by constellating your unique reading journey. I wrote this book to reimagine what a memoir is and all the worlds it could be, to take up space in our collective consciousness and to create a conversation that will span time, language and perspectives.

Throughout my process of finishing my dissertation and becoming a doctor (which my Ma still tells me is "not a *real* doctor"), I told myself that once I finished I would either visit Turkey or Cuba, two countries that have fascinated me since middle school when we had to research and present on various countries for a Social Studies unit. As soon as I completed my oral defense and walked across the stage at the doctoral hooding ceremony in the Spring of 2019, I flew off to Istanbul, Turkey for a ten day trip with a friend. I loved being able to travel without an agenda or detailed itinerary, a first for me. I took delicious cooking classes, full of flavors that reminded me of Indian spices yet mixed in new combinations. I took painting classes, learning traditional marble painting and learning how to make tulips out of paint on liquid surfaces and transferred onto paper. Tulips are indigenous to Turkey and often symbolize divine iconography and are a prominent motif in Turkish art. I was roofied at a gay bar and had a gold chain stolen. I was angry and scared once I woke up and realized what had happened. But I was grateful that I was not hurt and that I could replace material jewelry. This was a moment that reminded me of how quickly life can remind us of what really matters and what is worth worrying about. Coming back to the United States, I found no joy in my job. I soon left my job and decided to trust the Universe in a new path.

In September 2019, I packed a carry-on suitcase and decided to go on a trip to Cuba that has expanded into a five year nomadic journey across over thirty countries and most corners of the U.S. Going from a 2,000 square foot condo of three bedrooms on the Southside of Chicago into a small black carry-on of 1.26 cubic square feet was not intentional yet has been liberating beyond my wildest imagination. If you ever want to understand what possessions you actually value, try living with only what you can fit into a carry-on for a month. If that feels too intense and you don't live in a place like California, where the constant threat of an enormous earthquake means we have to always have an emergency bag to go ready in the car, try packing a small backpack or carry-on bag with just your essentials, toiletries, clothes, books, medicine, technology and luxuries of comfort. For me, the luxuries include a small tin of saffron and ground cardamom seeds along with black tea bags. Just a few things that transform regular black tea into a spicy and savory chai which makes even the noisiest airplane into a moment of homey comfort and peace. In these five years, I have started a consulting company, survived a pandemic, reignited my passion for art, published three coloring books and have experienced several wild adventures. While I have always wanted to write a book, these experiences have brought me to shaping this book you are holding right now.

When I talk to strangers and friends alike, they continue to ask, "How can you live without a home or always on the road?" It seems unbelievable to them that I am able to make money, secure housing, and still have a social life. I am beyond grateful for life skills that have allowed me the space to curate this life I had always desired but was worried it would be too "juvenile" of a vision. Humans began in this world as wandering foragers and I feel my little journey is a process of embracing this primal desire to be in balance with nature. What would you dream about if there were no limits? What would you do with your days if your basic needs were taken care of? What stories would you tell if there was no shame? What constellations would you create across the span of humanity? Queering Constellations is an invitation for all of us to question who gets to tell our stories, how and why they are told and where they are witnessed.

May the stars and spirits guide you on this journey.

www.ingramcontent.com/pod-product-compliance
Lightning Source LLC
Chambersburg PA
CBHW060923120626
46557CB00003B/853